See.
Faith.
Different.

Joel Holm

DEDICATION

To Marie

CONTENTS

ACKNOWLEDGMENTS

Thanks to all who encouraged me to write this book. The topics are common but hopefully the insights are fresh. Thanks for reminding me that although there is nothing new, there is much that needs to be continually renewed.

Introduction

For more than 2000 years Christians have been trying to define Christianity. Some works have held strong for centuries while hundreds, even thousands of books, come and go quickly. I haven't read thousands of these books but I've read enough to know that many say the same thing. And that is good for the basics of the Christian faith were never meant to be continually changing.

God loves this world. So, from that love, He desires a relationship with people He created to reflect His image. The foundation of Christianity is built off this one idea: God's love for His creation. Within this one idea are certain key building blocks of our faith. These building blocks receive a great deal of attention as they should. However the more air time an idea gets the more that idea can lose its distinctiveness.

These "basic building blocks of faith" (specifically, Christian faith) have continually come up in my thinking, writing and teaching. This book is an exploration of seven of them: chosen, grace, community, worship, prayer, scriptures, and service. This book is not an attempt to offer a broad, comprehensive breakdown of each area. But what I do offer is a seed, an idea, and a perspective to consider. *What if we look at it like this?* Does that fit? Is it true? Would it work? Would it help us understand and engage the truth better?

I would encourage you to approach this book as a series of seven pamphlets that can be engaged independently. Each chapter has an idea, and each idea has an actionable application for your life. Change happens one step at a time, and taking that next simple step is more important than having it all figured out from the beginning.

Like all of us who write about life and faith, I write as a pilgrim on the same journey. I write for myself as much as I write for others. After several decades of working through these ideas and perspectives, they still challenge my ways of believing, and they still push me to see faith different. I hope they'll do the same for you.

Joel Holm

Chapter One

Chosen: The Beginning of Faith

When I visited to California as a college student, a friend and I decided to attend a live taping of "The Price is Right".

In case you've never participated in this iconic celebration of American consumerism, here's a quick description of what happens behind the scenes. You line up in rows of five and appear before a producer, who asks you to guess the price of an item, like a microwave or a boat. Each person has ten seconds to answer. After everyone in your row has answered, you move on and let the next five people step up.

That's all you get. Ten seconds in front of a producer to prove you have that special something that it takes to be a contestant on their show. When it was my turn, I showed as much enthusiasm as I could muster over a hypothetical shopping experience, which is not much. Then the guy next to me, Tom, gave his answer, but with much more enthusiasm than I had.

You can probably tell where this story goes. When the announcer called the names of the contestants, I stayed in my seat while Tom cheered and danced his way on down, where he ended up winning a truck.

Most of us can remember the moments when we weren't chosen.

Maybe you weren't very athletic as a kid, and you remember how embarrassing it felt when the team captains picked back and forth, until one of the captains didn't so much pick you as get stuck with you. Or you remember the disappointment you felt when you tried out for a lead role in a school play but ended up with the role of "Villager" or "Townsperson." Or you remember the heartbreak you felt when a high school crush turned you down and went with someone else to Homecoming.

Maybe you remember feeling your heart drop as your eyes scanned the letter from that college you really wanted to get into.

Maybe you were recently one of five people up for a promotion, and you got passed over.

Even after we process the experience and move on, we still remember these moments. Because it *hurts* not to be chosen. If it's a situation that you don't have a lot of stake in, it merely stings; but if it's something that's important to you, or if it's anything relating to your identity, it cuts deep.

The opposite, however, is also true. There are few experiences more powerful than feeling chosen.

Simon Peter the Chosen Fisherman

In Luke 5, Jesus is teaching near the Lake of Gennesaret when the growing crowd starts to press into him. Two fishermen are nearby, washing their nets after a long day of work. Jesus gets into one of their boats and asks them to push him out a bit from the shore, where he sits down in his floating pulpit and continues to teach the crowd. One of the fishermen is a man named Simon, whom Jesus would later name Peter. When you read the story, you get the sense that Jesus had Peter in the corner of his eye the entire time he was preaching.

> And when he had finished speaking, he said to Simon, "Put out into the deep and let down your nets for a catch." And Simon answered, "Master, we toiled all night and took nothing! But at your word I will let down the nets." (Luke 5:4-5)

Notice how Jesus steps right into Peter's world of fishing and relates to him in that arena. And notice Peter's respectful, distanced response. Sure, he'll do what Jesus says to do. But he doesn't expect much to come of it.

Much to Peter's "astonishment," they suddenly catch so many fish that their nets start to break. Peter calls over some nearby fishermen to help, but there are so many fish that both boats begin to sink.

It's a strange, beautiful little miracle. No diseases were healed or lives saved, but Jesus catches the attention and the heart of Peter.

Peter's story illustrates two ways we can approach following Jesus.

The first is what I call, "The way of reservation." Like Peter, we respond to Jesus with caution and low expectations. We acknowledge who he is ("master"), but we're not expecting anything dramatic. We relate to him with honor and respect, but not with intimacy and passion.

Did Jesus choose us, or did we choose Jesus? We're not quite sure. That's why we have reservations. We're not so much passionately following Jesus as much as we are maintaining a mature agreement with him, in which he lets us do our own thing and we let him do his.

Those of us on this path are proper and appropriate. We know the right language, we know the routines, and we know the behavior. But we're more like actors than vessels. This path usually includes a sense of entitlement, and we refuse to feel unworthy. *Jesus kind of needs to help me,* we think, if only subconsciously. *That's part of the deal.*

After Jesus performs the miracle, Simon takes a sudden departure from this respectful, polite way of interacting with Jesus. He falls to his knees and says, "Depart from me, for I am a sinful man, O Lord." Whatever attitude he had when he reluctantly threw his nets over the side of the boat is broken, and he's suddenly overwhelmed in the presence of Jesus. He feels so broken, in fact, that he asks for isolation from him.

I had a friend in the Coast Guard who was on that first path with Jesus. He knew who Jesus was and identified with him. He tried to do the right things and tried not to do the wrong things, and doing so made him deserving of the gift of salvation. One Sunday he heard a missionary speaker share his story, and my friend was overwhelmed. He left church that day saying, "I've done nothing. I haven't sacrificed anything. I am such a sinner." He sounded like Peter.

Another friend of mine, a pastor, was out in public once with a group of people who didn't know him. They were all laughing and joking together. One of them asked what he did for a living, and without giving it very much thought, he lied. He didn't have the courage to tell them he was a pastor. He walked away from the conversation with a sense of shame. "Lord, I am such a sinner." Again, Peter's voice coming through.

There are moments when this response is fitting. But when that moment of regret and shame becomes a way of life, we can find ourselves on another path: the way of the perpetual sinner.

Are we perpetual sinners? That's not even up for debate! The Bible reminds us over and over again that all of us are sinners. But some of us can't seem to get up off the floor to follow Jesus because we're stuck there feeling broken and undeserving. We feel full of self-judgment and self-loathing. We compare ourselves to other Christians and feel unworthy. Every sermon we hear or Christian book we read sounds like some variation of, "God is good. I am not. I must try harder."

I believe there are three major ways people think about God. One: there is no God. Two: there is a God and I'm okay with him. Three: there is a God and he will never really be okay with me.

When we find ourselves in that third category, our response is usually one of extremes. First, we can seek isolation, like Peter requested, or like Adam and Eve attempted. Or the other extreme is we can become "alter-call junkies," constantly trying to fix ourselves, constantly asking others for prayer, constantly trying to solve our crisis of "I will never really be okay with God." If this is our identity as a follower of Jesus, it sets the trajectory of our faith. Whatever it is that we're walking towards, it sure doesn't look like hope or victory.

The other way

First, Jesus picks Simon's boat and asks him for his help. Then, despite Simon's skepticism and unbelief, he performs a miracle and gets his attention. Simon, realizing who Jesus really is, then falls to his knees out of shame, begging the Lord to depart from him. What does Jesus say next?

He doesn't say, "Well, I'm glad we've reached an understanding about who I am. Carry on fishing."

And he doesn't say, "That's right, you're a sinner. Try harder to get your act together."

Instead, Jesus says, "Do not be afraid; from now on you will be catching men." To which Simon Peter docks his boat, leaves everything, and follows Jesus.

Imagine how Peter must have felt in that moment, to be chosen.

In that culture, the fact that Jesus went around calling out people to leave their lives and follow him wasn't as unusual as it seems to us today. That's what rabbis did. They found people who they believed were qualified to job shadow them. It was normal to see a rabbi walking around, followed by twelve or fifteen men who were learning to be like him.

But for Peter to be called out of his fishing boat was highly unusual. In fact, for someone like Peter, to be chosen was astounding. No other rabbi would ever have chosen Peter; he didn't have any credentials. But Jesus chose him.

Later in his life, Peter would describe all of Jesus' followers as "a chosen people, a holy priesthood."

The way of the chosen runs directly between entitlement and shame. To identify as "a chosen people" inspires both confidence and humility. It's one of the many paradoxes of our faith. It's only *because* we were chosen that we have that worth—if not for him, we would have nothing. But the very fact that he chose us says that we are worth something.

Who does Jesus choose?

I have an exercise that I like to do with pastors in leadership trainings, where I stand in front of a whiteboard and pose a question. "What kind of people would you like to have serving on your ministry team?"

I usually start with one of my answers, just to get the ball rolling. I like to serve alongside people who are teachable. It makes my life easier, it makes their lives easier, and we can all go places together if we're teachable.

Then other pastors start throwing out their answers. We want people who are humble. We want people who are honest. We want people who are disciplined, wise, and mature. Then I draw a line and I say, "Now let's describe the people Jesus picked." Pretty quickly, a theme starts to emerge.

Jesus did *not* have a knack for putting together good ministry teams.

The people Jesus picked couldn't pray for an hour. They stole money from him. They were competitive. They were prideful. They were dense, particularly about metaphors. Sometimes it seemed like they didn't hear a word he said.

And yet Jesus would build his entire church on this less-than-stellar team that he put together—a church that would endure for thousands of years. What did he know about people that we don't? Jesus saw the potential in people, and he could look past their shortcomings and see into their hearts. He saw people not in terms of their past but their future, and he looked into that future and said, "I choose you."

Does everyone get picked?

Right after Peter leaves his boat and starts to follow, Jesus comes across a leper and heals him. This is Peter's orientation to life with Jesus: Touching the untouchables, reaching the outcast, choosing the forgotten. If any seed of pride had threatened to grow in Peter after Jesus chose him, Jesus weeded it out by immediately turning around and reaching out to a leper.

When it comes to our identity as one of God's chosen people, I think sometimes we are happy to see ourselves absolved and made clean. But how quickly we can accept our gracious gift and then start making evaluations about other people. "Me? I'm chosen. But I'm not so sure about them..."

Who God chooses has been a matter of church controversy ever since the book of Acts. In Acts 15, the leaders of the church came together to address a controversy over whether a Gentile must follow certain Jewish practices in order to be saved. The question they were essentially asking was, "Who's in, and who's out? And what do you have to do in order to be in?" The apostles and the elders met and discussed, and after a time, Peter got up and addressed them all, saying:

> "Brothers, you know that some time ago God made a choice among you that the Gentiles might hear from my lips the message of the gospel and believe. God, who knows the heart, showed that he accepted them by giving the Holy Spirit to them, just as he did to us. He did not discriminate between us and them, for he purified their hearts by faith… We believe it is through the grace of our Lord Jesus that we are saved, just as they are." (Acts 15:7-11)

Peter's answer to this question of whom God chooses was that *God chooses everyone.* He accepts everyone and does not discriminate—not because of anything we have done, but because of his grace. His will is that everyone might hear the message of the gospel and believe.

By the time the fourth century rolled around, the church was well established with five major centers: Antioch, Alexandria, Byzantine, Jerusalem, and Rome. Four of them were in the East, where they spoke Greek; Rome was in the West, where they spoke Latin. At this point, the East and the West didn't always get along. Both "sides" understood God differently, interpreted the scriptures differently, and did things differently. For example, if you wanted to be a clergy in the West, you had to be unmarried and celibate, but clergy in the East could get married and have kids.

Then in the eleventh century there was something called The Great Schism. Four bishops in the East excommunicated the bishop from the West, to which the excommunicated bishop in Rome said, essentially, "I can play at this game too; I'm going to excommunicate all four of you." So then there were two separate churches: the Orthodox Church, and the Roman Catholic Church.

The Roman Catholic Church continued to grow into the sixteenth century, where there lived a monk by the name of Martin Luther. The Catholic Church taught that in order to get to God, you had to go through the priest and pay for "indulgences." The church had essentially converted grace and forgiveness into a financial transaction. Luther didn't think that was right, and in 1517 he wrote ninety-five statements of his grievances against the Roman Catholic Church's teachings and nailed them on the main door at the Castle Church. Shortly after, scholars would distribute his list of statements all across Europe.

Suddenly there was a third church in the mix, the Protestant Church. Today we still have these three main Christian churches: the Orthodox Church, the Roman Catholic Church, and the Protestant Church. (Plus, of course, many denominations within).

The formation of the Protestant Church upset a lot of ideas that people had agreed on or been taught for years, and the question came up again. How are we really saved? Who is chosen? Does it have something to do with priests, or with church association, or something else?

Two theologians, John Calvin and Jacobus Arminius, arrived on the scene with their opposing answers to this question. Calvin said, "Listen, it's true that God chooses, but he doesn't chose everybody. God chooses those who are divinely elected." Arminius said, "That's not true. The Bible teaches that God wants everyone to be saved."

So, what does the Bible say on the matter? Does God want everyone to be saved? Is there something else going on? Look carefully at what Paul says in Ephesians 1:4-12:

> "For he chose us in him before the creation of the world to be holy and blameless in his sight. In love he predestined us for adoption to sonship through Jesus Christ, in accordance with his pleasure and will—to the praise of his glorious grace, which he has freely given us in the One he loves. In him we have redemption through his blood, the forgiveness of sins, in accordance with the riches of God's grace that he lavished on us...In him we were also chosen, having been predestined according to the plan of him who works out everything in conformity with the purpose of his will, in order that we, who were the first to put our hope in Christ, might be for the praise of his glory."

Who are these people? Who are the "we also"?

Verse four says that God chose us. Verse 5 says he predestined us. Verse 6 says he has freely given us grace. Verse 7 says we were also chosen. Verse 12 says we were the first to put our hope in Christ. Then in verse 13 he says,

> "In him you also, when you heard the word of truth, the gospel of your salvation, and believed in him, were sealed with the promised Holy Spirit, who is the guarantee of our inheritance until we acquire possession of it, to the praise of his glory."

Paul starts by saying, "As Jews we were chosen and we were predestined." All throughout the Old Testament, the Jews are described as "God's chosen people." Then he says, "As for you Gentiles: you were also included." This passage isn't about whether God divinely selects or doesn't select; it's about how whatever God was doing with his chosen people was also about *everyone else*. The Jews were chosen and predestined, and the Gentiles were chosen and predestined. This is the gospel, opened up wide, revealing that God's heart all along was for all people—that we, together, are a "chosen people, a holy priesthood."

Peter wrote in 2 Peter 3:9,

> The Lord is not slow in keeping his promise, as some understand slowness. Instead he is patient with you, not wanting anyone to perish, but everyone to come to repentance.

The Lord wants everyone to come to repentance. He created us to love us, and after we chose a path away from him, he offered a way back into his family. But we never stopped being his chosen creation.

I have a daughter named Lisa who we adopted from China. Once when she was about twelve years old, we were having a time of family prayer, and she said something that completely floored me. She prayed, "God, thank you that my mom and dad chose me."

As a parent I will never forget that moment. And as an adoptive son in God's family, I resonated with her words. I thought: *I should pray that prayer every day. Thank you, God, for choosing me.*

Why did my wife and I choose our daughter? We chose her to love her and to create a lasting, forever relationship with her. We didn't have a hidden agenda. We simply had the capacity in our hearts to love her and provide for her, and that capacity led us to choose her. That's why God chose us. That's why God chose *you*.

Once we're chosen, can we ever be dropped?

The story of Peter denying Jesus is one of the more heartbreaking stories in the New Testament, I think. When the rooster crows three times and Peter starts to weep, my heart sinks.

Three days later, after the resurrection, an angel at the entrance of the empty tomb appears before Jesus' mother and her two companions, telling them that Jesus is alive. The angel says, "Go, tell his disciples and Peter that he is going before you to Galilee. There you will see him, just as he told you."

Did you catch that? "Tell his disciples and Peter."

Wasn't Peter still a disciple? After what he did, Peter probably wasn't so sure about that anymore. But the angel makes it a point to say, "Make sure Peter gets the message, too." Peter is still chosen. He hasn't lost his identity *in* Jesus even after he denied identifying *with* Jesus. It's not what we do that defines us, but the fact that Jesus chose us.

The question underneath this, of course, is, "Can you lose your salvation?" I don't like the question because I think it's too small. If we're going to ask this question, why not ask a bigger question? *What is the best, truest, fullest way to live as God's chosen child?*

The best, truest, fullest way to live as God's child—the only way to live as his child, actually—is to abide in Christ. In John 15:5, Jesus says, "I am the vine; you are the branches. If you remain in me and I in you, you will bear much fruit. Apart from me you can do nothing."

Remember that bracelet "What Would Jesus Do"? The concept behind the bracelet was that you would be out in the world in these various moments of moral crisis—deciding whether to lie to your boss, for example—and then you'd look down at your bracelet and remember, "Oh right. Jesus wouldn't do this." Then you'd tell your boss the truth, having just dodged a sin bullet, thanks to your handy bracelet.

Is there anything wrong with asking what Jesus would do in your situation when you're making a decision? No. But the sentiment behind it leads us into a pseudo-version of abiding. Abiding in Christ is not about acing a series of on-the-spot moral decisions. Abiding is the work behind the scenes, before those moments of truth.

When we read the gospels, we have stories from only forty days of Jesus' life. Forty days! That's it! What did he do for the thousands of other days that he was on earth? Based on the glimpses that we have of Jesus' spiritual practices, he probably spent a lot of time in prayer, solitude with his Father, and reflection. Jesus, "the chosen of God" (Luke 23:53), abided in his Father and his Father in him (John 14:11).

When I was a teenager, everyone wanted to be like Michael Jordan. We bought the Michael Jordan shoes and we'd occasionally go to the court to try out some tricky, flashy shots. You know what we didn't do? We didn't get up at five in the morning and run five miles. We also didn't go to the court when no one was looking and shoot ten thousand baskets in a row.

Asking "What Would Jesus Do?" in an isolated situation is like asking, "How Would Michael Jordan Make This Shot?" Maybe I'll be able to get that particular shot into the basket. That's within my ability to do. But I can't be a professional basketball player without "abiding in basketball" anymore than I can be like Jesus without living in a constant, abiding relationship with him.

So how are you going to respond?

Imagine you're sitting in the audience on "The Price is Right," and you suddenly hear your name and the command, *"Come on down!"* What do you do next?

Do you weigh the pros of giving up your seat before deciding whether to sacrifice it? Do you ask for a few minutes to think it over? Do you consult with your family and friends? No. You run down because of what you might gain. You run down because you have been chosen. Paul didn't hem and haw when Jesus called him out of his chair. But later, after being beaten and thrown in prison, he counted what it had cost to give up his seat of comfort and power in life. He said his old life was *garbage* compared to the surpassing worth of knowing Christ and gaining him.   So how do we start? Where does the path begin?

However long you've been a Christian and wherever you're at in your walk with him, I think the real journey starts when you get one simple prayer down into the deepest part of your heart.

Thank you, God, for choosing me.

Life Application Question

1. What does it mean to you to be chosen by God?

2. How do you struggle to see yourself as chosen, always hoping He will approve of you?

3. If others are also chosen, how should that affect the way you see and treat people?

Chapter Two

Grace: The Bridge of Faith

I have had the privilege of walking across bridges on six different continents. I've been on massive bridges, small bridges, bridges with big pilings, and rickety bridges. But no matter how different one bridge looks from the next, they all serve the same purpose: to take you from one side to another.

We were designed for a world of perfection, but we live in a fallen world. As a result, all of us are trying to cross the distance between "how things are" and our intuitive, deep-down sense of "how things should be." On one side of the divide there is darkness, sin, death, and guilt; on the other side there is light, life, peace, and freedom. In other words, all of us are trying to cross from brokenness to wholeness. We try and we try to get there on our own, stuck in a constant cycle of self-improvement and failure.

Grace is the bridge. Grace is the *only* way over the chasm between death and life. It's a free and perfect gift, but the way across it isn't always easy.

In John 9, Jesus and his disciples have been in Jerusalem for about a week, and they've been having a pretty rough go of it. Their lives have been threatened and religious leaders have been challenging them. Then they come across a blind man. He doesn't know who they are, and he doesn't ask for anything. But the disciples stop upon seeing him and ask Jesus a theological question. Why is he blind? Was it his sin, or his parents' sin? What did he do wrong in order to put himself in this position?

Jesus stops them. Instead of answering their questions, he heals the guy. Without being asked, he takes some mud and puts it on his eyes, and then tells to man to go to the pool and wash it off. When he washes off the mud, he can see.

And then things start to get a bit strange from there.

When the man goes back to his village, people who have known him his whole life can hardly recognize him. Is this the guy who was blind? They don't understand how this could have happened, so he tells them the story of meeting Jesus. As he tells the story, everyone falls silent. What should have been a moment of celebration becomes a moment of fear. Why? Because Jesus had healed on the Sabbath.

The people go and get the Pharisees to weigh in on the situation, and the Pharisees get really upset. They don't see the miracle; all they see is a broken rule. The Pharisees question the (formerly) blind man, who says, "Listen, I don't know what happened or how it happened, but Jesus healed me."

Then the Pharisees go to the man's parents.

Can you imagine? This man's parents must have mourned their son's situation for years, but now they're in this predicament. If they celebrate the healing, they'll get kicked out of their community. So in a tragic moment, they turn to the Pharisees and essentially wash their hands of the situation, telling them to talk directly with their son. You can only imagine the pain and the anguish that must have gone through this man's mind and heart as his parents betray him.

The Pharisees go back to this guy and ask him again: what happened? Now he starts getting bold, almost a little angry. He says that Jesus healed him, and that Jesus had to have come from God in order to do it. At this, the Pharisees kick him out. Now that this man has his physical sight, he is removed from his community and completely alone.

It is at this moment that Jesus reappears into the story. He finds the man and asks him, "Do you really want to see? Do you know who the Son of Man is?" The man who was blind becomes a worshiper of God.

What a strange, messy, incredible story of grace. Grace is not as simple as "God does great things and everyone is happy." When you really experience God's grace and choose to live in God's grace—when you cross the bridge—it will open your eyes and heal you and offer you true life. But it will also challenge the way you were living in profound ways.

Grace shines. Look at what Jesus says in John 9:4. "As long as it is day, we must do the works of him who sent me. Night is coming when no one can work. I am the light of the world." The disciples are trying to make sense of this chaos and they approach this man's situation from a completely theological position. "Why is this guy blind? How do we make sense of this? How do we make this right?" We do the same thing. We feel like we are trapped in darkness and we want to know how to make sense of it, how to categorize it, how to avoid it, and how to fix it.

Jesus stops the disciples and says, "Look, you've got this all wrong. The world is a strange and dark and it's getting stranger and darker. While we are here, our job is to bring light." Jesus did not engage in a discussion with them about the blind man. All he did was go and heal him.

A while ago I heard the story of a single mom of a teenage boy who was stabbed and killed in a fight. When she got the call, she was devastated. She had so many questions, and her unanswered questions turned to bitterness.

Time went on, and the young man who committed the murder was convicted of manslaughter and sent to prison. After about two years of living in bitterness and torment, the mother of the slain son was told by a Christian friend of hers, "You need to go visit that man who killed your son." She said, "I could never do that." But her friend urged her that she needed to do it if she wanted freedom from her bitterness. She needed to let grace in.

The mother eventually became so desperate for some sort of breakthrough that she decided to go. When she showed up, the prisoner was so shocked she was there that he didn't want to go see her at first. But eventually he agreed to meet her, and they sat across a table from each other. Very few words were spoken during that first meeting. The next month she went back, and it was still quiet and awkward. But something compelled her to keep coming back. It was during the third meeting that she looked across the table and said, "I want you to know that I forgive you for killing my son." The man literally fell onto the floor weeping. Grace broke through. She came back month after month over the next few years and they actually built a relationship that was centered on grace.

After completing seven years of his prison sentence, the man had the chance to go before the parole board. But because he didn't have a family or a place to live, no one really believed he would get parole. He stood in front of the board knowing he would be rejected. But on the day of the parole board meeting, this mom showed up. She stood next to the man who killed her son and spoke to the parole board about the relationship they had developed over the past few years. She told the parole board that he could come live at her home and she could be his mother. The man got his parole and moved into her home. It had been so many years that the community didn't even recognize him as the man who had murdered this woman's son.

Grace changes you in such a way that you are not even recognizable as the same person.

The story of God's grace starts in Genesis, with Adam and Eve. They are given everything except this *one thing* that God tells them they can't have. To get that one thing, they reject all of God's blessings and go and hide in darkness. But God comes and finds them and says, "No, come into the light. We can still be together." The story of God's grace continues all throughout scripture. Moses rejects his calling and runs away to the desert, but God shows up in the light of a burning bush, saying, "Come closer, Moses." When God sends the ultimate gift of grace, Jesus, he leads the wise men to the stable by the light of a star. Paul was a persecutor of the church and beyond any hope; the light of grace knocked him off his horse and turned his life around. Grace shines.

But here's the problem. This bridge of grace is meant to take us from darkness to light. But if we are in darkness and we don't believe there is a bridge of grace for us, we begin to deny that we are actually in darkness. We have to make our darkness look like light. And our world is extremely talented at packaging darkness as light. We can take something dark and destructive and wrap it up until it looks like something completely different than what it is. Free choice, personal expression and harmless fun become cover-ups for sin.

Grace without sin is arrogance, because it accepts all the blessings but denies the need for a savior. But sin without grace is absolute hopelessness. You can pretend that what you're living in is light for a time, but after a while you learn that you're trapped.

So what is this bridge of grace? How does it work?

When my daughter was in college, there was this week when she went away and was without email for the week. She had her own separate bank accounts but it was linked with my account, so when she got a notification from her bank saying that she had overdrawn her account, I got the same notice. She didn't have access to her email, but I got the email, and I knew that she was going to be penalized. As soon as I saw the notice, I went online and transferred some money to her account. An automatic email then went out, saying that her account had been balanced and that she wouldn't be given a penalty.

Two days later she got home and read the first email, and she freaked out. Then she immediately read the second email and saw it had already been taken care of. This is what the Father has done for us. Before we even knew there was a penalty to be paid, Christ paid it for us.

Grace is a free and amazing gift. But it's also incredibly confrontational. Why did Jesus heal on the Sabbath? Why couldn't he have waited a day and avoided all of the mess that man had to suffer in exchange for his sight? Can you imagine Jesus' disciples watching what he was doing and thinking, *Really, Jesus? Didn't we just have our lives threatened by the very guys who you're about to tick off again? He's been blind from birth—can't this wait eight hours?*

But Jesus healed the man on the Sabbath to confront their understanding of law and grace. We look at the situation and think, "How could the Pharisees be so blind?" Jesus restores a man's sight and completely changes his life, and all they can see is that he broke a rule. It seems ridiculous. But we do this, too. When grace shines in a way that doesn't look completely fair and just to us, we get upset. When a parent hands two kids some candy and one gets slightly more, the kid who gets slightly less doesn't see the gift of the candy in his hands anymore; all he sees is that he got ripped off. Jesus tells a parable about a master who hires two people at different points in the day then gives them both equal pay. The person who worked longer calls out, "That's not fair!"

There is a friend of mine whom I invested a lot of time in. I mentored him and gave him some great opportunities, and I was expending a lot of time and energy to build into him. Then I found out through someone else that my friend had made some bad decisions that affected me negatively. My friend went to other people for help and seemed genuinely sorry for what he had done; I heard that he repented and received grace and moved forward with his life. But he never came to me about it. I remember hearing what was going on, and part of me kept thinking, "That's just not fair. He's moving forward in grace and freedom, but he never came and spoke to me. I'm the one who was hurt and betrayed."

When grace shines, it confronts the part of us that wants everything to be just and fair. The law that we're holding it against is God's law, fulfilled by Jesus—so there's nothing about grace that isn't fair. But if we're honest, sometimes we want the bridge of grace to be a bridge of rules. Rules are something we can control.

After I had finished with third grade, I went to a four-night-long summer camp. Over the course of the first three nights, the camp leaders drilled into me what a bad third grader I had been, and I felt pretty guilty about it. So on the fourth night when they gave the alter call, I responded. I wanted to go to heaven. I wanted to commit my life to Jesus. I prayed the prayer, and then the leaders of the summer camp commissioned me to go out and live like a good Christian.

Honestly, I tried my best, but I wasn't perfect. So when I came back to summer camp at the end of my fourth grade year, I spent the first three nights feeling guilty again, and then responded to the alter call again on the fourth night. This happened again and again all throughout my grade school career. That's the cycle we go through when we don't have a correct understanding of grace and law. We think that it's by grace that we're saved but that it's by law that we "stay saved." Which means that if we break the law, we have to start the process over again. But the process will never change until we understand that we're saved by grace and that we remain in Christ through grace. It is "not of ourselves." The salvation isn't our work, and the justification isn't our work. It's all grace.

The author of Hebrews says in chapter 13, "You hearts should be strengthened by God's grace, not by obeying rules."

There are many things you'll need to earn in this life, but God's unending love is not one of them.

There is, of course, plenty of opportunity to misunderstand this. In the Old Testament, God gives his people 613 rules to abide by. In the New Testament, we're given more than twice as many rules. Grace is not the absence of rules; grace gives meaning to the rules. For the Pharisees, the rules were the ultimate aim in life, and everything that they did was in service to the rules. For Jesus, the rules served a purpose rather than being the purpose. By tampering with the rules, he revealed that his highest purpose wasn't to follow the rules but to glorify God. The law was never the means of gaining God's love but about our response to his unearned love.

Maybe you've read the book *Les Miserable*, which was adapted into a Broadway play and later into a movie. The story is essentially built around two characters: Javier, an officer of the law who makes sense out of his life by following and upholding rules, and Val Jean, who is a picture of redemption. Van Jean had been in prison for nineteen years and was let out on parole. While he's on parole, he's mocked and abused and can't get a job. A priest finds him at his wits end and welcomes into his home to feed him. But Val Jean is trapped in darkness and can't escape, so in the middle of the night he steals expensive silver from the priest's home. Sure enough, he's caught by officers of the law and is brought back to the priest, who now has a choice: law, or grace? In an incredibly powerful scene, the priest goes back into his house to get more items for Val Jean and says, "Here, you forgot to take these."

The law doesn't transform people. Grace transforms people. And at various moments in our lives, all of us will be offered a choice: grace or law? The mother of the slain son was given that choice, and she chose grace. Jesus was given that choice when religious leaders threw a prostitute in front of him and said, "What's it going to be, Jesus? Grace or law?" He wrote something in the ground that we as readers don't get to see, and then he invited anyone without sin to cast the first stone. He chose grace. A few chapters later, the parents of the blind man were given that choice, and they chose law. Why? Verse 22 says, "His parents were afraid of the Jewish leaders who decided that anyone who acknowledged Jesus as the Messiah would be put out of the synagogue." They chose the law because they were afraid.

When you have the opportunity to show grace to someone who you think is unworthy of it, you get a glimpse of what God has already done for you. You will never be asked to show more grace than what has been given to you. Titus 2 puts it this way: "Grace teaches us to live in the present age in a right way that shows we serve God."

When we're at a place where we're being confronted by grace, our prayer should be, "God, grant me grace in this situation so that I can grant grace." God gives us grace so that we can lead others to grace, and ultimately to Jesus. Consider how grace worked in the life of the blind man. At the beginning of the story he refers to Jesus as "the one they call Jesus." In the middle of the story he refers to him as a prophet. Later in the story, he says Jesus is from God. At the end of the story, he becomes a worshiper of the Son of Man. Grace empowers us to be worshipers of God. When we're struggling in darkness, we lose the ability to worship God, but when grace shines its light on us, we're delivered from blindness and can see and worship Jesus clearly.

If you're in a situation right now in which you're in need of grace yourself or in need of granting grace to someone else, I want to end with this encouragement.

Sometimes the bridge of grace feels very rickety. Now, I don't mind walking across rickety bridges when they're a few inches off the ground and just keeping my feet from getting wet. But when I'm suspended high in the air, it's a little more nerve-wracking. The same is true when we're offering grace or in need of grace in high stakes situations. Sure, grace sounds great. But when we're afraid, we are tempted to prefer walking across a solid bridge of rules than a rickety bridge of grace. The more we can practice walking across the bridge of grace in our day-to-day life, six inches off the ground, the more we'll be able to step onto that same bridge with confidence when we're suspended mid-air. If you're walking across the bridge of grace right now, lean on Corinthians. "My grace is sufficient for you. My power is made perfect in your weakness." The bridge will hold if you'll walk across it.

Life Application Questions

1. Why is grace so hard to embrace unconditionally?

2. How can you begin to walk across the bridge of grace?

3. Who can you lead across the bridge of grace?

Chapter Three

Community: The People of Faith

My ministry travels often take me to China, where I've sat in the presence of underground church leaders. It is always an overwhelmingly humbling experience. When I look into the faces of these men and women of faith who have sacrificed so much and who have put everything on the line for the sake of Christ, I'm torn between taking off my shoes because I'm standing on holy ground, or else keeping them on and leaving because I don't belong. Instead I sit there with them, a humbled misfit among heroes.

I have that same feeling when I read the names and stories listed in Hebrews 11. Noah. Abraham. Isaac. Jacob. Joseph. Moses. You look at this list and see an ark in the midst of a great flood, the father of our faith, a prophetic dreamer and ruler of a nation, and the waves of the Red Sea parting. That's not the end of it. After recounting these and many more stories, the author of Hebrews writes, "I do not have time to tell of Gideon,

Barak, Samson and Jephthah, about David and Samuel and the prophets, who through faith conquered kingdoms, administered justice, and gained what was promised; who shut the mouths of lions, quenched the fury of the flames..." The stories go on and on.

None of these people were perfect—the heroes of the Bible are all flawed in some way. But still, when I look at this list, I get that same feeling as when I'm sitting among underground church leaders. *I don't belong here.*

And yet there in Hebrews 11, listed among all these giants whose stories we've heard over and over, there is one name that catches our attention. "By faith the prostitute Rahab, because she welcomed spies, was not killed with those who were disobedient."

Noah. Abraham. Moses. The prostitute Rahab. Remember that song from Sesame Street? *One of these things is not like the other. One of these things just doesn't belong.* At first glance, Rahab the prostitute is a total Hebrews 11 misfit. Even the way she's listed makes her stand out. Why is she called "the prostitute" when the other names are given without any kind of title or explanation? I think the author of Hebrews didn't want us to gloss over the fact that God can do incredible things through any person who has faith, no matter how qualified or unqualified or *vastly unqualified* he or she is.

In truth there is only one hero in all of the stories in Hebrews 11. *God is the hero.* In every single story, he shines through. He's the one preserving his creation in the ark when it deserved total ruin; he's the one giving Joseph dreams and positioning him in leadership; he's the one parting the Red Sea and shutting the mouths of lions and quenching the fury of the flames. He's the one who is redeeming all that is broken and hopeless in this world.

And if there is any person who was acquainted with brokenness and hopelessness, it was probably a prostitute in Jericho.

Rahab's story is a story of God's redemptive work.

The only part of Rahab's story that we have an account for is in Joshua chapter 2, at the pivotal moment in her life. Two spies, sent by Joshua to survey the land, find their way into her home. The king of Jericho finds out and sends word to Rahab, telling her that she should turn in these two men; but instead of doing as the king tells her, she hides them and tells the king that they've already left. After the king's men leave, she goes up to the roof where she had hidden them. She tells them that she knows who they are, and that she knows the God they serve is "God in heaven above and on the earth below" (verse 11).

Across all times and cultures, prostitutes have always been on the undignified outskirts of society. And from what we can tell from a couple contextual clues, Rahab wasn't just a prostitute; she also ran a brothel. Suddenly the king of Jericho sends a message directly to Rahab. A person of power reaches out to her for help. If I were Rahab, I imagine this would seem like an opportunity…if not a monetary opportunity, than at least a chance to attain some self-dignity and clout for being useful and helpful to the king.

But Rahab had heard rumors of God's people and of the powerful things their God had done. Maybe she had heard stories about how some Egyptians went with the Israelites when they were delivered out of Egypt, and she might have gathered that Israel's King welcomed outsiders. Maybe she even glimpsed the underlying truth, which is that his kingdom was ultimately *for* outsiders—that when his kingdom was fully established, there would be "no Greek or Jew, no slave or free, no male or female," but rather unity and equality.

But whether or not she senses any of that, what she does know was that her life is in danger. She knows that the Israelites are going to try to conquer Jericho. Maybe if she obeys the king's orders and turns in the spies, then the Israelites' attack will be thwarted, and her life will be spared.

But Rahab decides to align with a different kingdom than the one in Jericho that didn't give her any hope.

She lies to the king of Jericho—a dangerous move—and then strikes a deal with the two spies. "Please swear to me by the Lord," she says, "That you will show kindness to my family, because I have shown kindness to you. Give me a sure sign that you will spare the lives of my father and mother, my brothers and sisters, and all that belong to them—and that you will save us from death."

Rahab realizes that it's only with this king that she has any hope. She identifies with God, like many of us have. But Rahab doesn't just identify with the king. She identifies with the kingdom and with the community.

If you want to identify with God, you have to identify with God's people.

It's incredible how much of life we do in secret. The easy parts of faith, like worshiping or celebrating, we do in public. Yet the hardest parts we do in secret. We struggle in secret and we hope in secret, trying to work things out with God so that we can save face with everyone else. But it doesn't work that way. It's God's power alone that heals and redeems us, but he does all this in the context of community.

Being forgiven is different than being healed. If you've ever been caught in a cycle of struggle and sin, then you've experienced this. You ask God to forgive you and you know you're cleansed, but soon enough that same sin occurs again. You've been forgiven, but you haven't been healed.

I once had a couple come to me for marital counseling, and they confessed that they had been really angry with each other over the previous few months. They were fighting constantly, and they knew their relationship wasn't honoring God or each other.

I said, "That's great!"

They looked at me like I had lost my mind. What kind of a Christian counselor was I?

I clarified, "Coming to me and confessing this means that you're ultimately more concerned about honoring God and each other than you are about self-image. You've repented, but now you're ready for healing and victory. This is a great place to begin."

James 5:16 says, "Confess your sins to one another that you may be healed." Confession is key to our healing, and it only happens in relationship and community. Why is that?

When it comes to sin, we have three dynamics at work.

We have "holiness," which is living our lives in a way that honors God. We have "sin," which is making choices that don't honor God. And then we have a third element, called "temptation."

We look at temptation as a bad thing, when it's neither bad nor good. It is the opportunity to sin, but it is not sin. Oftentimes we feel shameful about temptation, thinking that if we were really living a holy life that pleased God, we wouldn't even have the temptation to sin. But temptation is merely a crossroads in the paths of sin and holiness. When we're at the crossroads, we have a chance to look down the path of sin and decide whether to go down it or not.

The problem is that most of us are pretty bad at seeing past our noses. We're good at figuring out what we want to do in the present moment, but we're not good at looking three months ahead at the consequences of our actions. Other believers—even other believers who aren't very good at seeing past *their* own noses—are however very good at helping us see past ours. This is the beauty of God's design for an interdependent body of Christ.

We all need each other. Confessing our sins to one another and sharing the temptations we're facing is one of the ways (maybe the most effective way) that God provides a way out from under temptation. God gives us each other not just so we can be healed of our sins, but to help us out of sinning in the first place.

Sometimes we get to a point in our sinful brokenness where there's only one option: run.

The question is where, or who, we'll run toward.

> Before the spies lay down for the night, she went up on the roof and said to them, I know the Lord has given you this land and great fear of you has fallen on us, so all who live in this country are melting in fear because of you. We have heard how the Lord dried up the water of the Red Sea for you when you came out of Egypt and what you did to the two kings of the Amorites who were beyond the Jordan, to Sihon and Og, whom you devoted to destruction. And as soon as we heard it, our hearts melted, and there was no spirit left in any man because of you, for the Lord your God, he is God in the heavens above and on the earth beneath. (Joshua 2:8-11)

You would think Rahab would say, "We were so scared, and we ran away." She is terrified and overwhelmed, but instead of running from the God she's terrified of, she runs to him.

The same thing happened to Moses. Moses decided he was going to do God's work out of his own effort, but he failed and ended up in a wilderness, hopeless and despairing. God showed up and Moses was overwhelmed and a bit terrified, but he chose God because he knew God was at work.

It happened to David. David, the king of Israel, committed adultery with Bathsheba. If you want to see how much despair he had, read Psalm 51 and you will see a man who has lost everything. God showed up and David was overwhelmed and terrified. But he could see God was at work, and he chose to follow after God.

It happened to Peter. Peter denied Jesus and ran off into the night, hopeless and in despair. Despite his shame and disappointment in himself, when given the chance, he realigns himself with Jesus because he knows Jesus is at work.

We have to identify with God, identify with his people, and identify with his work.

I was born in a Christian home. I had good Christian parents who taught me about the love of God. I was aware of the Gospel story of God's grace, but it hadn't permeated my heart. So when I got to my teenage years, I began to do good things to prove myself to God. I began to perform for God. I was a *good* person doing *good* works trying to be *good*. The more I tried to perform my way to justification, the more I made my identification with God about my work and not his work, and the more hopeless I became.

To identify with God and his work, some of us need to repent of our sins, but some of us need to repent of our virtues. Jesus taught that if we think that doing good is going to get us access to God, we're actually in worse condition than the sinner.

Rahab identifies with God's people and with God's work.

Then the story takes a twist. Rahab sees an opportunity to not only save her own life but to help others.

> Now then, please swear to me by the Lord that you will show kindness to my family because I have shown kindness to you. Give me a sure sign that you will spare the lives of my father and mother, my sisters and brothers, and all who belong to them and you will save us from death. (Joshua 2:12-13)

If you're going to identify with God, you have to have the courage and faith to identify with God's purpose for your life. Rahab had hope that God would save her family, but she had no idea the extent to which God would use her. Her one act would save not only her family, but also the entire world.

The story of Rahab hiding the spies is the only account we have of Rahab's life. But in the genealogy in Matthew, we learn that Rahab ends up marrying one of the spies that she hid on the roof, Solomon, and together they have a son, Boaz, who marries Ruth. They have a son named Obed, who has a son named Jesse, who is the father of King David. Rahab the prostitute is the great, great grandmother of King David. She is a direct ancestor of Jesus.

Do you know what we would do if we had a Rahab the prostitute in our family tree? We'd find a way to hide her. We take the skeletons of our family tree and put them in the closet, but do you know what God does with the skeletons? He breathes them to life and he gives them new purpose. He didn't stuff Rahab into the shadows. He put her on the very first page of the New Testament.

Various church historians have been uncomfortable with the idea of Rahab the prostitute being in the genealogy of Jesus. Some have tried arguing that the Rahab in Matthew was a different Rahab than Rahab the prostitute, or that "Rahab the prostitute" was actually just an innkeeper. But the writers of the Bible never tried to blot her story out. James points out, "Was not even Rahab the prostitute considered righteous for what she did…?"

Why isn't she listed as "Rahab the prostitute" in the genealogy of Jesus? Because that was no longer her identity. In the community of God's kingdom, Rahab has a new identity.

Your identity is not the worst part of your story.

There's a member of my church named Kim. Kim is an amazing person and she has been a member for a long time, but if you'd met her a few years ago, she wouldn't think so. When she was nineteen, she became pregnant by her boyfriend and they got married, making a bad situation worse. What began as verbal abuse turned into physical abuse, and then he forced her into drugs and she became a drug addict. She told me that there were many nights where she would sleep outside in the bushes, naked, because he would strip off all of her clothes at gunpoint and force her out of the house. She knew she had to get out of there and she knew she had to protect her children, but it seemed like every time she thought of getting out, he knew about it and would threaten her. He told her that if she left, he'd kill her and the children. She knew he was serious. One day she found herself with a baseball bat in her hand, not knowing what to do as he attacked her one last time. She knew she had to take the risk to get out.

Fast forward a few years, and she meets a man named Mark. They get married. But the demons of her past continue to haunt her because she is forgiven but not yet healed. Someone invites her to our church, saying that it is a place of healing. Kim says that the minute they walked into the building, she knew they were home.

Her and Mark realized they needed help, so they went to a ministry we host called Celebrate Recovery. Good people helped them and ministered to them and gave them compassion, love, and mercy. After graduating out of Celebrate Recovery, they went through our church's leadership college, where they learned the Bible and graduated with honors. When she went on her first missions trip to Uganda, she was nervous, but the leaders on the team supported her and coached her and had faith in her.

Kim has now been on four missions trips to Uganda, and she coaches and supports new people who are nervous about going. Kim is now one of the key leaders in the Celebrate Recovery ministry, where she ministers to people and guides them through healing and restoration. She's become one of the key members of our church.

Kim's story is a story of God's redemption. Kim's redemption, like Rahab's and all of ours, took place through community.

Kim has a brand new identity. If Kim were listed somewhere in the Bible, she wouldn't be listed as "Kim the teenage mom" or "Kim the drug addict." She'd be simply "Kim."

Rahab continued her negotiations with the spies.

> The men said to her, "We will be guiltless with respect to this oath of yours that you have made us swear. Behold, when we come into the land, you shall tie this scarlet cord in the window through which you let us down, and you shall gather into your house your father and mother, your brothers, and all your father's household." And she said, "According to your words, so be it." Then she sent them away, and they departed. And she tied the scarlet cord in the window." (Joshua 2:17-21)

It could be days or weeks before they return, but before they even leave the city gates, Rahab is tying that cord. She doesn't hesitate. She makes her stand.

Where is your scarlet cord tied? What do you identify with? How do you want to be known? Do you want to be known by your career, accomplishments, or bank account? If you want to identify with God, you have to take a stand and tie your scarlet cord the way Rahab does. She identifies with God's people; she identifies with God's work; she identifies with God's purpose for her life; and she takes a visible stand so that she can be identified as one of God's own.

What's your story? Do you see God as the hero of it? Do you identify with his people, his works, and his purpose for your life? And have you made your stand? If Rahab the prostitute belongs in Hebrews 11, there's space for you, too. You belong in a place of victory and healing and faith, which is available in the community of God's kingdom.

Life Application Questions

1. How do you identify with God and His people?

2. When are you tempted to run from God?

3. How has grace given you a new identity?

Joel Holm

Chapter Four

Worship: The Intimacy of Faith

It's a common misunderstanding within Christianity that in order for something to be deep, it needs to be complicated. In reality, the more we complicate something, the further we get from the truth. Keeping things simple and uncluttered is the real art and work of going deep.

The path Jesus gave us to a deep relationship with him is actually a simple one. Whenever you feel yourself lost and wandering in your faith, you probably need to go back to the basics of worship, prayer, study, and service—all within the context of community. We're going to explore aspects of these principles throughout the rest of this book, but the first one we'll examine is worship.

There are many scriptures that talk about worship—what it is, how we do it, and so on. I like Psalm 150. To read and agree with it *is* worship, and then we can examine it for what it teaches us *about* worship.

> Praise the Lord. Praise God in his sanctuary; praise him in his mighty heavens! Praise him for his mighty deeds; praise him according to his excellent greatness! Praise him with trumpet sound; praise him with lute and harp! Praise him with tambourine and dance; praise him with strings and pipe! Praise him with sounding cymbals; praise him with loud clashing cymbals! Let everything that has breath praise the Lord! Praise the Lord!

Psalm 150 answers five questions about worship: Who? What? Why? Where? How? Let's look at each one.

Who do we worship? What is worship?

The Psalmist starts by saying, "Praise the Lord." The "who" in this is clear; we're worshipping the Lord. But what does it mean to worship the Lord?

Worship is the act of ascribing ultimate value to something. When you ascribe ultimate value to something, that thing will drive and transform your life. This is true no matter what you choose to attribute value to. If you worship your career, your career will drive and transform your life. If you worship a person, that person will drive and transform your life. We can put massive amounts of time and energy into earning money or achieving fame or becoming successful, and each of those things will transform our lives. But will we find it to be a life of depth and meaning? No. The "real life" is only available to people who attribute ultimate value to God, setting all of those other things—success, family, work, relationships, and so on—in their proper place.

Here's the best way I can illustrate how the act of attributing value to something can change your life.

Shortly after my wife and I were married I decided to buy a piece of art for our home. We had recently settled into our home and I had saved enough money to buy a real painting. I spent $400 on an oil painting without knowing much about the artist or the painting. For some people, $400 may be a lot of money for a painting while for others, it may be a small amount. For me, at that time, it was a huge amount of money. I framed the painting and hung it on our living room wall. I enjoyed the painting but over the years it became very commonplace. Once we moved into a house for just a year and I didn't even bother to put it up. In our next house I put it up again but often forget it was even there. However one evening I was waiting for my wife to get ready to go out and for some unknown reason I decided to look up the artist of that painting. What I discovered changed my view of that painting and my treatment of it. It had been more than ten years since I bought the painting. I learned the artist had died and since her death the painting had increased greatly in value. It was now worth more than $4000. Immediately my value in the painting changed. Now when people came over to our house, the first thing I showed them was the painting. I treated the painting with great care and respect. Something that had little value now became of great value to me.

There's an interesting story in the book of John (chapter 14), where Philip is asking Jesus to show him the Father. Jesus says, "Don't you know me, Philip, even after I have been among you such a long time?" Philip is one of the people in Jesus' inner circle. He's traveled with Jesus, he supports Jesus, and he's committed to Jesus…but he still didn't *know* Jesus and ascribe him with his true value. You can be wrapped up in all the activity of Christianity and know everything there is to know about Jesus and still not have the most important part straight, which is knowing him on a personal level and worshipping him as God.

There are two ways to know someone: informational and personal. If I want to know you from an informational standpoint, all I need is for you to accept my friend request on Facebook. I can get all of your basic information there, as well as some things that you've said and pictures of places you've been. But if I want to actually get to know you personally, I'll need to spend time with you. You'll have to tell me about your life. You'll have to open up to me. And I'll have to tell you my story and what makes me tick. There will have to be openness and sharing and connection.

It's as if Jesus was saying, "Listen, be careful, Philip. It looks like you have all the information secondhand. You may not even really know me."

Until you answer the question of who Christ is, none of your other questions are going to be answered. They all hinge on the person of Jesus and your personal relationship with him. You can't approach Jesus philosophically or theoretically or intellectually; you have to approach Jesus relationally. The philosophical, theoretical, and intellectual information about Jesus will fall into place only once the relational level is in place, which happens in worship. When you discover who Jesus is, personally and intimately, then the truth becomes open to you.

Worship shifts an informational knowledge of Jesus to a personal experience with Jesus. When we try to get to know Jesus on an informational level, it's usually out of a need that we have. We want God to provide something for us. But true worship is about offering ourselves to God, not about getting something out of God. "Therefore I urge you, brothers and sisters," says Paul in Romans 12:1, "in view of God's mercy, to offer your bodies as a living sacrifice, holy and pleasing to God—this is your true and proper worship."

Worship isn't something you do to feel better about yourself or to get something you need in order to make your life work. Worship is about surrendering yourself to the Lord no matter how you feel, regardless of whether your life is "working" or not. We read the story of Paul and Silas worshipping while shackled in prison and think it is such an amazing story, but I'll bet they didn't think much of it. I'll bet if we asked them why they were worshipping, they would say, "Because we exist. Its what we were created to do."

One of the most profound moments I've ever experienced happened when I was in an Eastern European country ministering to gypsy children at a feeding project. I sat next to an eleven-year-old girl and, through a translator, started asking questions. I asked here if she attended school. She said no, so I asked why she didn't go to school. She told me that she had to work every day, and I asked what kind of work she did. She said, "My brothers and I go out and try to find food for our family." In that country, at the end of every block, there are large garbage bins with holes into which you stuff your garbage. She explained that as she was the smallest one in the family, she was the only one who fit into those holes. Her brothers would lift her through the hole and she would have to forage and fight with rats to get food for the family.

My heart ripped in half when I heard that story. I didn't even know what to say. I felt hopeless when I heard that story. Then the food project volunteers came and took away the empty plates, and a pastor got out his guitar and began to play a worship song. I watched this eleven year old girl who fights with rats for food lift her hands in the air and begin to worship God with the biggest smile on her face.

Worship has absolutely nothing to do with our circumstances and everything to do with who we are. We are creatures of God who were created to worship. Worship has nothing to do with our needs, our emotions, our wants, our style, our preferences, or anything else. It has everything to do with him.

Who do we worship? We worship the Lord. *What is worship?* Worship is ascribing God with ultimate value. *Why do we worship?* We'll go into this question in more depth, but the simplest answer is that we worship because we exist. It's what we were created to do.

Why do we worship?

Verse 2 says that we worship God "for his acts of power, for his surpassing greatness." We worship because compared to everything else there is nothing else.

Whenever I go to a new country, I always buy a map for my collection. At the center of each of the maps I've collected over the years is the country in which I bought it.

We all think of ourselves as the center of the universe.

It's funny, really, because the universe gives us absolutely no indication that we're the center of it. There are millions and millions of galaxies in the universe. If the galaxy we live in were the size of North America, then our solar system would be the size of a quarter. We can't measure our galaxy the way we measure our lives on earth, with yardsticks and mile markers; we have to measure with light years. And this is just our galaxy—one of millions that God created. The earth? It's not even at the center of our solar system. You could fit 1.3 million earths into the sun that we orbit around, which is just an average-sized star of millions of stars in our one solar system that is part of our galaxy, which is one of millions of galaxies.

I'm not trying to make you *feel* small. I'm trying to convince you (and me) that we *really are* very small. Compared to the greatness of God's creation, we are small. Compared to his surpassing greatness, which is greater than all of his creation, we are *so, so* small. Our view of ourselves is vastly bigger than we are in reality, and our view of God is vastly smaller than he is in reality.

The vastness of the universe shouldn't be depressing and overwhelming; it should be inspiring. There is no greater feeling than getting a glimpse of his surpassing greatness and our remarkable smallness, especially when we consider that God knows every single hair that is on our heads. We are part of an indescribable, cosmic-scaled intimacy with the creator of a universe.

The only response to that is worship.

How do we worship?

Look at the list the Psalmist gives us. "Trumpet, harp, lyre, dancing, strings, pipe, symbols."

It's interesting that over half of this psalm of it is dedicated to "how." Who, what, where, why are all answered, but over half is dedicated to the specifics.

In the ancient world there were basically three categories of instruments: instruments that you hit, instruments that you blew into, and instruments that you would strum. All three are listed in this psalm. That doesn't mean very much to us now, but in ancient times, these were radically different styles of music, and this psalm could have generated controversy. *What do you mean worship God with strumming? Don't you know that blowing is the only true way to make music and worship to God? This category can't be right…*

By listing these different categories of instruments, the Psalmist is saying that worship is not about a particular style. The type of instrument that's used isn't what qualifies it as worship. If it's offered as worship, it counts as worship. Don't spiritualize a style and don't make worship selfish. Worship is about the Lord, not us.

And yet if you listen to us talk about worship, a lot of what we talk about is style and personal preference. If we were to rewrite this Psalm to fit our culture today, perhaps it would sound like:

"Praise him with freestyle dance and orchestra music; praise him with the organ and electric guitar; praise him with a church choir and a full band…" And now, suddenly, this is a "controversial" Psalm for our day. I know a few people who would take issue with some of those forms.

It doesn't matter which form of worship you prefer. What matters is that you don't spiritualize the form of worship that you use to worship God, or devalue the form of worship that someone else uses to worship God. There is nothing about any instrument or movement that is inherently more spiritual than another. God invites us to worship him with all of it.

Where do we worship?

Psalm 150 says that we praise the Lord in his sanctuary, in his mighty heavens.

One day I was biking along the beach and I noticed that people were staring at me. They were openly and rudely staring at me, actually, and I couldn't figure out why. Then one of my headphones fell out of my ear and I suddenly realized that I wasn't so much quietly humming under my breath as I was singing very loudly. By myself. On a bike.

You can worship wherever you are, but worship has an inherently communal aspect to it. "The sanctuary" is where God's people gather together to worship. Worship is a time of private connection with God, but there is also a horizontal, corporate aspect to worship. To put it another way: worship is a personal experience that happens in the context of community.

Did you know that the second most frequent command in the Bible is to sing? The first one is to pray, but the second one is to sing. Why is it so important to sing? Ephesians 5 days, "Be filled with the Spirit declaring to one another with Psalms, hymns, and songs from the Spirit."

A few months ago I hit a wall of discouragement in my life. I was waiting to get medical results on something alarming, and one of my best friends was in the hospital after a boating accident. I came to church on a Sunday morning feeling beaten down and discouraged, and I sat next to a man in our church who happens to be one of the loudest singers I've ever encountered. I was standing during a worship song, not really engaged, and suddenly his voice bellowed out next to me. He was so close and so loud that it felt like he was singing directly to me, or over me, proclaiming these powerful words of faith and worship. My voice started to pick up, and soon I joined in…quietly at first, and then a bit louder. This is horizontal worship. God uses you to inspire others to worship. Together we make a joyful noise unto Him.

Sure, we can worship with headphones on while riding a bike on the beach, but there's a community aspect to worship that's absolutely necessary, and that's part of how we're designed as worshippers.

Why start with worship?

Why does a church service always start with worship? And why start a discussion about spiritual disciplines with worship instead of prayer or study?

We start with worship because worship is what sets everything else in its proper order.

Worship answers all of the essential questions in life. *Who am I? Why do I exist? Why am I here?* Ephesians 1:11 says, "Because of what Christ has done, we have become gifts to God that he delights in, for as part of God's sovereign plan we were chosen from the beginning to be his."

Without worship, everything else becomes twisted. If you study the Bible without worship, study will become about acquisition of knowledge. If you pray without worship, prayer will be about leveraging God to get what you want. If you evangelize without worship, evangelism will become about recruiting people to a religion. Whatever you do without worship can be become self-focused. Worship is necessary.

Who are you? You are a gift to God. Why are you here? You are here to worship God. There are many other facets to your existence, but the simplest and deepest one is that you are here to worship and glorify him.

Life Application Questions

1. What is worship to you?

2. Why do you struggle to worship God at times?

3. How can you enhance your worship to God/

Chapter Five

Prayer: The Power of Faith

God has given us many paths toward him, which are called disciplines. There are what I consider the primary disciplines of worship, study, prayer and service; but there is also disciplines such as solitude, meditation, fasting, and many more.

Most Christians gravitate toward certain paths and not others. For examples, some find journaling to be a rich way of going deeper with the Lord, while other people find it a chore. Does every Christian need to journal? No. If you hear God's voice better when taking walks through nature, then put down your journal and go take a walk.

However, there's a good case to be made for disciplining ourselves in the primary paths of worship, prayer, study, and service. The Bible hammers away at these four so much that it's hard to say, "Well, if you're just not "feeling" like a study of the bible, then don't bother with God's Word. Take a walk through nature instead." God's Word is so foundational to our walk as Christians that not abiding in it is going to have a negative effect on our lives. The same is true for worship, prayer, and service. We can take creative license with other disciplines, but these ones are foundational.

For me, worship and study have always come pretty naturally. I discipline myself to do them, but I generally find them easy and fulfilling.

Prayer, however, has always been another story. It's not that I *don't* pray, because I do. It's simply that prayer feels like labor in a way that study and worship do not. It's not something that flows out of me, and it's not something that always leaves me feeling refreshed and deeper in step with the Lord.

Typically when I try to improve my prayer life, I think of ways that I can discipline myself more. I commit to waking up earlier, or praying for longer periods of time. That usually works for a little while, but it doesn't change the fact that prayer remains a difficult discipline for me.

Recently, however, I decided to approach my prayer life in a different way. Instead of renewing my commitment to pray for certain periods of time, I said, "God, I want to go deeper in my prayer life with you. I want to commune with you." I didn't want to simply check off "prayer" on my list of spiritual activities. I sincerely wanted something deeper and richer, whatever that looked like.

Shortly after I prayed this prayer, I was reading the third chapter of Ephesians, and I came across a scripture that gave me clarity and vision for what my prayer life could look like. Paul is writing to the church in Ephesus, and he's describing how he prays for them. Let's take a look at each verse.

Verse 14: "For this reason, I kneel before the Father."

Earlier in verse 12, Paul says that we have an opportunity to approach God with freedom and with confidence. The opposite of freedom and confidence in the context of prayer would be *obligation* and *timidity*, which is the picture we usually have of someone approaching a king on his throne. But Hebrews 4:16 says that we can come "boldly to the throne of our gracious God." For the simple reason that God has made himself available to us in prayer, Paul kneels before the Father.

Verse 16: "I pray out of his glorious riches that he may strengthen you with power through his spirit in your inner being."

Paul doesn't start by praying for external issues or circumstances. He doesn't say, "I pray that you will have enough food to eat," or, "I pray that you will have enough money for your basic necessities," or, "I pray that you will be safe and healthy." Those were tough times for Christians in Ephesus. Why didn't Paul start with something a bit practical?

Take a quick inventory of your prayer list. How many of our prayers are for something we need God to do, heal, or provide? And how many of our prayers are for our *inner being?* We pray for a change in our circumstances and for peace in the midst of difficult circumstances, but how often do we pray that God would strengthen us to withstand our circumstances?

Maybe the most practical thing Paul could do was pray for the inner lives of his brothers and sisters. It's like the difference between hoping for smooth waters and making sure your ship is in seaworthy condition. Which is really more practical—hoping to avoid waves, or maintaining your ship?

My daughter had been dating a guy for about a year before they announced their engagement. My first few prayers for my daughter and future son-in-law went something like, "God, will you bless them with a great engagement that's full of joy." But after a couple of those prayers, I had to stop. I didn't know what was best for them. Maybe they would be better off if their engagement period was spent fighting and butting heads and getting everything out on the table before the commitment. Who knows? So I began to pray, "God, would your Holy Spirit strengthen and empower them in their inner beings, so that whatever circumstances they face, they aren't going to fall apart, but they will be strong knowing you are present with them." Something in my spirit deepened when I prayed that prayer, in a way that it hadn't when I was praying for smooth-sailing.

Verse 17: "...so that Christ may dwell in your hearts through faith."

In verse 14, Paul kneels before the Father—not out of ritual, but in confidence and freedom. In verse 16, Paul prays for a strengthened inner life. In verse 17, he prays for *presence*.

There are two main things that make us doubt God's presence: suffering and sin. When we go through difficult times or experience tragedies, the first question is always, "Where is God in all of this?" And nothing makes us feel more lonely and isolated than sin.

Paul prays that Christ may dwell in their hearts "through faith." Often we have to rely on faith, not on our feelings, to sense God's presence. If we rely on our feelings and our feelings aren't picking up any kind of "God signal," we quickly become hopeless. But if we have faith to lean on, we'll know that God is present with us even when it doesn't feel like it.

I spent the first eighteen years of my life growing up as a missionary kid in South Korea, so when I moved to America, I experienced massive culture shock. I spoke English, but I knew absolutely nothing about American culture. When I went to the mall, I would bring a calculator with me so that I could calculate the exchange rate of the currency to decide if the purchase was worth the value of what I was paying.

When you're going through culture shock, which is a kind of trauma, you get a bit squirrely in your brain. I lost the plot for a while. I didn't know what I was going to do and I couldn't make sense of my life, so I dropped out of college.

All throughout that year, my mom was praying for me. She could have prayed, "God, help Joel get a job," or, "Help him with his finances," or, "Help Joel so that he doesn't get into drugs." Those would be very appropriate things for a worried mom to pray, and maybe she did pray those things. But she told me later that her core prayer was, "Christ, make your presence known to Joel, so that he knows he is not alone."

A few months after dropping out of college, I was sitting in my living room in the townhouse that I shared with two guys, who weren't there at the time. Out of the blue, Christ showed up in a way that I couldn't even describe. I spent ten hours on the floor weeping tears of joy and faith. I stood up after those ten hours, and I knew what my life was about. I knew who God was and what he had called me to do. My mom could have prayed, "Help Joel get a job," but instead she prayed, "Make Joel fully aware of your presence." What an immensely more powerful prayer.

Verse 18: "I pray that you, being rooted and established in love, may have power together in all the Lord's holy people to grasp how wide and long and high and deep is the love of Christ. And to know this love that surpasses knowledge."

This part of his prayer—"to know this love that surpasses knowledge"—is very interesting coming from Paul, because Paul was a knowledge guy if there ever was one. He lived and breathed knowledge. He was a straight-A kind of student who rose up through the ranks. He would have been the summa cum laude of any seminary. No matter how many times I read the book of Romans, I have to stop every five sentences to unpack it because it's so thick and rich with theology. The book of Acts shows us that Paul loved to debate intellectual philosophers, and he had no problem challenging and testing them. He was definitely a knowledge guy.

But in verse 18, he tells us that there's something even greater than knowledge. *Love surpasses knowledge.* Jesus didn't send his son because he had a good idea and a logical solution; he sent him because he *loved* us. The Bible says that three things remain: faith, hope, and love. Knowledge isn't anywhere on that list of things that remain, and of the three that do, love is the greatest.

Where is love experienced? Love isn't experienced on an intellectual level, but on an emotional level. What is love if it's not felt in some way? Sometimes you'll hear people separate the "knowing" and the "feeling" of love. As in, "I know my dad loves me, but he just doesn't show it." In other words: "I can rationally accept the idea that my dad loves me, but I don't feel like it." When you hear someone say that, you can bet there's some damage in that relationship. Love needs to be felt, not merely conceived of. Paul prays that we wouldn't simply rationally accept the idea of God's love, but that we would actually grasp the height and width and depth of the fullness of God's love for us.

A few years ago I officiated a wedding with a particularly emotional groom. As we were standing at the front waiting for the bride to show up in the back, he started sobbing. Truly, sobbing. He wasn't crying stoic groom tears—he was crying buckets, and his bride hadn't even shown up yet. I stared at him in disbelief while a more thoughtful person handed him a handkerchief. When he actually bent over sobbing, I thought, "Man, you gotta get your act together. She's not even here yet. This is so awkward."

When she finally showed up at the end of the aisle, he absolutely lost it. But as soon as the bride looked into the eyes of her blubbering groom, all the way from the other end of the aisle, her own eyes filled with tears. As she walked toward him, they looked at each other with this unbelievable expression of love and intense emotion. What started as a really awkward moment transformed into a truly beautiful one.

It could have gone another way. What if he was blubbering at the end of the aisle, overwhelmed with love and joy, and then she sauntered around the corner and walked toward him like it was no big deal? Some of us walk down the aisle like an indifferent bride, sauntering through life like Christ's love isn't anything to get all that worked up about. We haven't grasped Christ's immense love for us.

We adopted our daughter Lisa when she was just a few months old. Toward the beginning of the adoption process we were given a picture of her, and in the months leading up to meeting her, we looked at that picture and we prayed for her. We prayed, "God, if she doesn't get all the food she needs, she'll be okay. If she doesn't have the right kind of shelter, she'll be okay. But God, would you somehow show her your love? Would you somehow wrap yourself around her, protect her, and impart to her a deep sense of your love? We can't be with her as her parents, but we trust you to love her for us."

We went to China to pick her up when she was about six months old, and during the first night we were there at the hotel with her, we heard a knock on our door at about midnight. We opened the door to find a Chinese woman, weeping.

What we didn't know when we adopted Lisa was that she had been selected to be part of a foster program, which was very unusual. What was even more unusual was that her foster mom would show up at our hotel at midnight, which was firmly against the rules. But she said she absolutely had to check on Lisa. As I watched her weep over our little daughter, I knew God had answered our prayers.

Lisa had been deeply loved when we had been helpless to show her love.

Before you pray for resolution or provision or understanding, pray for an understanding of God's love. Paul says it surpasses everything else.

Verse 19: "I pray that you might be filled to the measure of the fullness of God."

Paul didn't pray that the people of Ephesus would experience "a touch" of God. He prayed that they might be *filled to the measure of the fullness of God.* This is an authoritative, confident prayer.

When my son was in high school and college, I used to pray that God would surround him with good Christian influences so that he could grow in his faith. But later I began praying for the fullness and the authority of God in his life, so that *he* could be an influence on the people around him.

I think sometimes we're timid in our prayers because we don't want to make it too hard for God to show up.

"Lord, will you *just*…"

"God, we *just* ask that…"

As in, *we're not asking for much here, God. Just*…

Paul didn't pray for "just" anything. He asked for full measure.

Verse 20: "Now to him, who is able to do immeasurably more than we can ask or imagine according to his power that works within us."

Many Christians have what I call a "probably-not" mentality in prayer.

We ask God to do something, but when he doesn't answer immediately, we start to think, "Eh, probably not." Most of us won't say "probably not" out loud, but in our hearts and minds, that's what we think. Pretty soon we stop praying for the probably-not items altogether—like long-term illnesses, or a parent who is far from God, or a cycle of sin that we can't break out of—and we stick to things that we think will more than likely work out, whether God intervenes or not. It's like a defense mechanism for our faith.

But Paul takes a jackhammer to our probably-not mentality and defense mechanisms, and he prays this big, confident, faith-filled prayer. "Now to him who is able to do *immeasurably more* than we can ask or imagine…"

Having adopted two kids, my wife and I have been very involved with helping other adoptive families. A few years ago I came in contact with a pastor in Australia, and I found out that he and his wife had a desire to adopt. Unfortunately, adoption in Australia is an even more tedious and expensive process than it is in the States. This pastor friend said to me, "Yeah, we would love to adopt a Chinese baby, but probably not."

I asked, "What did you say?"

He said, "We'd love to adopt, but probably not."

I said, "I have a verse for you." I had him look up Ephesians 3:20 and say it out loud. *Now to him who is able to do immeasurably more than we could ask or imagine according to his power that works within us.* Then I said, "Let's say it together." *Now to him who is able to do immeasurably more than we could ask or imagine according to his power that works within us.* Then I said, "How about you memorize it."

A few months later I visited Australia again, and I asked him how it was going on the adoption front. He said, "Eh, not much to report." I gave him a small donation to get him started and asked him to repeat the verse again, which he did, half-heartedly. *Now to him who is able to do immeasurably more than we could ask or imagine according to his power that works within us.*

Three and a half years later, I got an email.

I opened the email to see a picture of this Australian pastor, his wife, and their adopted Chinese daughter. I immediately called him, and as soon as he picked up I said, "Wait a second, what was that verse again?"

If you have a probably-not list, put this verse in front of you. Read it. Repeat it. Memorize it. Maybe you've had a desire in your heart to adopt but you've thought, "Probably not." Maybe you've had a dream for a ministry, but you've stopped pursuing it because you think, "Probably not." Maybe you've asked God to heal a long-term illness but you've stopped praying about it because you think, "Probably not." Get rid of the probably-not list and start praying to a God who is able to do immeasurably more than we can ask or imagine.

Verse 21: "To him be glory in the church and in Christ Jesus throughout all the generations forever and ever amen."

Where does Paul land this big, authoritative, hopeful, faith-filled prayer for the people in Ephesus? He lands on the kingdom. He ends his prayer by pointing us to the bigger picture: God's glory in his church and to the generations. The big picture gives context for our individual lives.

Do you want a richer prayer life?

Paul's prayer isn't a seven-step formula. It's a focus. If you want to cultivate a richer prayer life, don't aim to pray *longer*, aim to pray *deeper*. That simple shift in my perspective on prayer has been transformational for me.

God has invited us to approach him in freedom and in confidence. For that reason, let's kneel before him.

A strong spiritual core is practical and necessary for meeting the challenges of life. So before we pray over our challenges, let's ask God to strengthen our inner being.

If suffering and sin are the two greatest threats to living in an awareness of God's presence, the opposite is also true. An awareness of God's presence in our lives is the greatest aid in our suffering and the greatest threat to our sin. So let's pray for that indwelling presence.

Do we really grasp the heights and depths and lengths of God's love? Would we feel different if so? Would we live different? Let's find out, and let's pray for a stronger grasp of God's love for us.

Are we settling for a half portion of God when his fullness is available to us? Let's pray that we would be filled to capacity with the authority of God.

When our probably-not list gets bigger, our faith gets smaller. Let's dump the list and pray for the big faith items, knowing that we pray to a God who is able to do immeasurably more than we could ever hope or imagine.

And finally, let's turn our focus to the big picture of God's kingdom.

Let me start by praying this over you.

I pray that out of his glorious riches, he may strengthen you with power in his Holy Spirit and inner being, so that Christ may dwell in your heart through faith. I pray that you, being rooted and established in love, may have power together with all the Lord's holy people to grasp how wide and long and high and deep is the love of Christ...and to know this love that surpasses knowledge, so that you may be filled to the measure of all the fullness of God. And now to him who is able to do immeasurably more than all we ask or imagine according to his power that is at work within us. To him be glory and the church and in Christ Jesus throughout all generations forever and ever. Amen.

Life Application Questions

1. How can you broaden your prayer life?

2. What parts of prayer are a struggle for you?

3. Who can you invite to join you in prayer?

Chapter Six

Scripture: The Truth of Faith

What would happen to your body if you only had one meal a week?

Say it's a really good meal. Say it's packed full of protein and vitamins. Say it's the most well-rounded, nutritious meal that could ever be served on a plate. You eat it slowly and digest it well. And then you don't eat again until the following week.

How long could you go on like that? The human body can endure a lot for a short time, but long-term? First you would feel weak, and then your organs would begin to shut down. Your vision would blur, and then your immune system would weaken, leaving you susceptible to all kinds of attack.

How many Christians live on this meal plan, spiritually? They go to church and get one really good meal. They take it in, meditate on it, and perhaps respond to it in some way. Then they go home and fast until their next meal the following week. What happens to the spirit? How long can it endure malnourished?

Jesus uses "food language" to describe our spiritual need for sustenance. In Matthew 4:4, when he's responding to the enemy's temptation to eat, he says, "Man shall not live on bread alone, but on every word that comes from the mouth of God." The word is our food as Christians, and life comes from consuming it. It's our source of energy. It's how we were designed to thrive. It's how you stay strong enough to ward off attacks.

So what does digesting the word do for you? How does our spiritual digestive and nutrition system work? Psalms 19:7 tells us how the word functions for our spirit, saying, "The word of the Lord is perfect, refreshing the soul. The testimony of the Lord is trustworthy making wise the simple." The word does two things. First, it resuscitates you and brings life and breath back into you. Second, it gives you wisdom so you can be healthy and thrive.

If a starving person gets a good meal, that meal is going to start the process of resuscitating his system and bringing him back to life. But being saved from starvation is different from being healthy and strong. Eating that initial meal is how he'll be saved from death, but eating regularly is how he'll become healthy. In the same way, hearing the word and believing is how we are saved, but digesting the word regularly will make us healthy and functional in life.

My daughter and I like to go scuba diving together. Once we were diving in Mexico, and for whatever reason my tank ran out of air, which is a really scary thing when you're a hundred feet below the water's surface. I swam to the guy who was set up with an extra breathing mechanism, and he handed it to me. How good it felt to breathe again. Do you feel short of breath, spiritually? Do you feel like there's a weight on you? Do you feel like your tank is out of air and you're grasping around under water? Open the word. In 2 Timothy 3:16 it says that all scripture is *God-breathed*. Opening scripture when you're spiritually short of breath is like swimming over to a breathing mechanism when you're a hundred feet under water.

Try this exercise. Simply read the following passage of scripture at the same pace as you breathe in and out, just as a way of making a connection between spiritual breathing and physical breathing.

> I sought the Lord, and he answered me; he delivered me from all my fears. Those who look to him are radiant; their faces are never covered with shame. This poor man called, and the Lord heard him; he saved him out of all his troubles. The angel of the Lord encamps around those who fear him, and he delivers them. Taste and see that the Lord is good; blessed is the one who takes refuge in him. Fear the Lord, you his holy people, for those who fear him lack nothing. The lions may grow weak and hungry, but those who seek the Lord lack no good thing. The eyes of the Lord are on the righteous and his ears are attentive to their cry. The righteous cry out, and the Lord hears them. He delivers them from all their troubles. The Lord is close to the brokenhearted and saves those who are crushed in spirit. The righteous person may have many troubles, but the Lord delivers him from them all. (Psalm 34)

His word gives us breath. It resuscitates. But the word does more than simply sustain us; it also gives us wisdom.

There is a difference between knowledge and wisdom. I learned this lesson a few years back when my wife was having a party with ten of her friends. It was winter, and they had all brought coats, which Marie put on our bed. The party was going late and I needed to go to bed, but my bed was covered in coats.

Here's what I knew: there were coats on my bed, and I needed to get them off so that I could sleep. I also knew there was a bench by the front door, which would be the most logical place to put the coats. I had all of that information and knowledge in my head, and I acted on it. I picked up the coats and walked down to lay them on the bench. Suddenly ten women were looking at me with confused looks, and I froze. The only face that didn't look confused was my wife's—hers was crystal clear. I knew exactly what was going through her mind when I saw that look. But what could I do? I just sighed and set the coats down and went quietly back upstairs.

Sure enough, a few minutes later, all of the women had left the house, and I went downstairs to talk to my wife. "What were you doing, Joel?" she asked. "They all thought you were telling them to leave." I had knowledge, but I didn't have wisdom in that situation.

God doesn't just give us knowledge through scripture; he gives us wisdom. But how does he bring wisdom?

Hebrews 4:12 says, "For the word of God is alive and active. Sharper than any double-edged sword, it penetrates even to dividing soul and spirit, joints and marrow; it judges the thoughts and attitudes of the heart."

The word of God is active. The stories and letters and prophesies and poetry—all of it is alive. The people in the Bible are alive and active, too. Hebrews 11:4 says that Abel still speaks even though he is dead. What does that mean? How is he speaking?

Years ago I was getting ready for bed in a hotel room in China when I heard a knock on the door. I opened it to a woman who looked about thirty, and I assumed she was with the concierge service of the hotel. She asked me if my room was okay, and I said that it was and thanked her for checking on me. Then she asked if I was alone. I thought that question was a little personal, but figured she was going to get me a fruit platter or something else that required a portion size, so I said that I was alone. Then she asked me if I wanted a *massage*. I knew she was not referring to the kind of massage that was good for my health.

All of a sudden, Joseph from the Old Testament runs naked right past me, stopping long enough to say, "Joel, come with me." Joseph is alive and speaking even though he is dead. I've meditated on his story enough that when a moment in my life coincided with a moment in his story, he was alive and speaking to me. I looked at the lady and said, "You know what, I have a friend who's almost here. I have to go."

In another season of my life I was struggling with disappointment. You know those seasons where things don't work out the way you thought they should? Things don't fall into place, which surprises you, because you've told God everything he's supposed to do but he doesn't do it? You remind him of it every day and it still doesn't happen?

I was in a season like that, sitting in the corner of my office on the floor. Suddenly I looked to the other corner and there was Paul and Silas. They were sitting in the corner of my office and they didn't look so good. They were in chains and had blood all over them. Paul looked at me and said, "Joel we're going to sing. Do you want to join us?" I looked at Paul and I asked, "How can you sing? You're in prison." Paul looked back and said, "It's just what we do. We are made to worship God." Sitting on the floor of my office, I raised my hands and began to sing and worship God, and I felt a burden lift. Paul and Silas had ministered life to me.

The word of God is alive and active. It meets you where you're at and offers breath, life, and wisdom.

But the word does something else a little more serious and a little more difficult. The word *judges* and *penetrates*. It gets to places in you that you can't even get to. It puts a finger on those thoughts and attitudes deep down.

I remember one time I was thinking about some of my friends who were doing some incredible things in ministry, and I thought, "I haven't done enough." I wanted to do more for God. I wanted to have greater vision for God. Later I was reading through the book of Philippians, and I came to the verse that says, "For me to live is Christ." That word hit me in a different way and in a deeper place than it had before. I realized that I wanted to do something that looked significant to God instead of desiring to be intimate with Jesus. That verse exposed something in me that I wasn't even aware of.

When my brother and I were little we had this spy test kit that came with invisible ink. We would write messages on paper with this ink and then put on these special glasses so that we could read it.

Our lives are like a blank piece of paper that don't make any sense until we look at the through the lens of God's word. Through His word we discover what is happening in our heart and what God wants to do in us.

So, we know that digesting the word is important. It resuscitates us. It gives us life. It sustains us. It judges and penetrates.

But Jesus makes another very interesting statement in John 4:34: "My food," he says, "is to do the will of him who sent me and to finish his work." His sustenance comes not just from consuming the word but also from *doing* the word of God and from finishing his work.

I was reading an article out of a medical journal that talked about a research study regarding "acts of kindness." The article mentioned how, when you do something kind, a chemical is released in your body, which makes you healthier and happier and gives you a better outlook on life. God has connected the spirit and the body in such a way that when you do what the word says, it makes you stronger and healthier. Jesus said that his sustenance came from *doing* the will of God.

If we're honest, Christians are best known for what we *don't* do. But that's not where our strength comes from. The word has power when we read it like disciples. Not like Pharisees, who read only for data. Not like fanatics, who read only to feel something. But as disciples, who read for direction and purpose and instruction.

Maybe you're familiar with the story of the woman with the issue of bleeding who fights through the crowd to touch the hem of Jesus' garment. Why the hem? This woman was familiar with Malachi in the Old Testament. In Malachi there is a prophecy that talks about the coming Messiah, saying that when this Messiah comes, there would be healing in his wings. The English word translates to "wings." But literally it means "the fringes of his tassels," or his "hem." It's the same word that's used in the story of the woman touching the hem of Jesus' garments.

This woman knew the word and she read it like a disciple. She did the word. And when she touched his hem, Jesus stopped in amazement at her faith.

In Mark 4:25 Jesus says to his disciples, "Consider carefully what you hear... With the measure you use it, it will be measured to you—and even more." He's saying: it's up to you. How much do you want to get out of the word? How much life and insight and truth and fullness do you want? Whatever you apply, you're going to get back. He's talking about faithfulness: seeing something through from beginning to end, from hearing to applying to completing.

When my daughter graduated from college, I brought a cap of my own along to throw in the air. I figured that since I had paid for all four years of her college, I should celebrate finishing! So, when all the graduates threw their caps in the air, I threw mine. There's a sense of strength you gain in finishing something that God gives you to do.

A few years ago I read this very interesting verse in Psalms 119 that says, "Seven times a day I praise you." At that time I was so busy with my life that I could go seven hours without thinking about Jesus at all. I read this verse and I digested it, but then I had to do it. So I set my cell phone to go off seven times a day for three months. Seven times a day my alarm would go off on vibrate, and it would remind me to acknowledge Jesus' presence and to express my love and gratitude for him.

After three months, remembering Jesus was with me became part of my daily life. Years later, I can't go an hour or two without thinking about Jesus or communicating with him. I don't need my phone alarm anymore. That particular work was completed in me. I have a lot more stuff to work on, but there was something that was fulfilled that brought strength to me.

No matter how good the meal is, it's not good enough to last you a whole week. You have to learn to feed yourself. You have to open the Bible and read it, digest it. And then you have to live it out, because that's where the nutrition and energy comes from.

I use the acronym R.E.A.D. as a helpful way to remember the process of thriving on God's word.

R: Ready

It's been said that how you spend your day is how you will spend your life.

If you don't make time in your day to read the word, then the word is not going to be a part of your life.

This is far too important to just wing it. You have to have a plan. The enemy may not be able to destroy you, but he can distract you. Even if you have the desire to get into the word, unless you have an intentional plan to do so, things will always "just come up," and before you know it, three or four weeks will have gone by, and you will still be living off one meal a week. So you have to plan this out with a great deal of intentionality.

A few years ago I was flying in a small helicopter in India. There had been a helicopter crash a couple weeks prior on that exact route, so I was a little nervous, waiting for something to happen. Sure enough, about halfway through the flight, we flew into some clouds and a little red light began to beep on the instrument panel. But what made me even more nervous than the flashing red light was when the pilot took out a manual and starting thumbing through it to figure out why the light was blinking. I was thinking, "Really? This is when you're going to read the manual?"

Don't wait until the red light is blinking to read the manual. God in his goodness responds to us in crisis, but let's have better stewardship over our time and energy and focus when we're not in crisis mode.

When should you plan to read? Let's give God our best time of day, not our leftovers. My wife is at her best at six o'clock in the morning. Me? I haven't had my coffee by six, so six isn't a great time for me. My best time with God is after I've gotten ready for the day and had my coffee. What's your best time? Don't waste that optimal time in your day on something of lesser importance.

E: Encounter.

This is like the difference between scarfing down a meal and experiencing a meal. When my daughter told me that she wanted to get into the word more, I suggested that she pick a New Testament book, read a few verses a day, and then write out in her own words what she thought it was saying. That's a great way to engage and encounter the word, not just read it.

Reading the Bible is a big part of my job description, so I've done it a lot over the years. But I'm always noticing new things that surprise me. Once I noticed this verse in the Old Testament where God says that every new king of Israel must write God's law in his own hand. I thought that was a unique law. A king has scribes and all kinds of servants, so why should he do this one task?

There's something about engaging with the word instead of just reading it or knowing it that makes a difference. The verse struck me in such a way that I started the practice myself. I would write five or six verses out and then journal what God was teaching me through them. That act forces me to slow down and read the words at a pace that I can digest them. Remember when your mom told you to slow down and chew your food? Same idea. You have to do the work of digesting.

A while back I was asking God for wisdom on a decision I needed to make. One morning during my devotions I copied down the parable Jesus told about a master who gave his servants gold and told them he'd check later to see how fruitful they had been. I'd read this parable many times, but as I was writing it down word for word, it dawned on me that the master never told his servants what to do with the gold. I realized how much freedom their master gave them. It was so freeing for me in that moment of decision-making to hear God communicate that I should do what was on my heart. *Do what I've gifted you to do,* I heard him say through this passage. *Let's see what you come up with.*

If you're struggling to find depth in reading the word, it could be because you're reading it but not engaging with it. Engagement makes the difference.

A: Apply.

It's not enough to agree with God; you must obey God. Everyone agrees that Jesus is a great teacher, but it's something else altogether to obey him. As C.S. Lewis said, "Everyone thinks forgiveness is a wonderful idea until they have someone they need to forgive." If you really want to see the word take root, and if you want to thrive spiritually, you have to read the word like a disciple. Read it for understanding, and then—most importantly—apply it.

There's a woman in my church who is very strong in the word. She teaches Bible classes and spends a lot of time engaging with the word intellectually, but also as a disciple. Once she was parking her car at the grocery store when another car ran into her. It wasn't her fault at all, so she was planning to get out and graciously get the person's contact information. But to her surprise, the at-fault driver got out of the car screaming and yelling at her. The driver who was at fault was absolutely livid, even though she had no reason to be as the accident was her fault.

Most people wouldn't know how to respond to a situation like that. Depending on their fight or flight instincts, one person might meekly try to get the other driver's information while another person might start yelling back. But this church member knew what to do. She remained quiet and let the other driver yell for a while. Then she began to speak words of kindness and gentleness to her. She began to speak words of care and concern over her life. Believe it or not, before they even got around to exchanging information, she was praying with this other driver.

She knew the word and she applied the word. What strength comes from merely knowing the word? None. The strength comes from knowing the word, in this case "a gentle answer turns away wrath", and then applying it. In doing so, like this lady did, you will drive away from that situation not upset or angry or in a bad mood, but fresh out of a ministry experience.

Jesus said that his food came from doing the Father's will. Without this step in the process, you'll never get to…

D: Discover.

If you have a hunger to know God and to experience the full life that Jesus came to offer us, the good news is that you can have it. He's already given it to you. But unless you intentionally engage with and apply the word, you'll never get to truly discover it.

I was in China a few years back teaching a group of about thirty underground church leaders, which is as covert and dangerous as it sounds. If we had been caught, I would have been expelled but they would have gone to prison.

These thirty pastors oversaw a movement of eight million Christians. Because we were meeting in secret, our location was this little old house that was closed up with no ventilation. It was summer and was very hot. We were teaching four days in a row, from nine in the morning till nine at night. These church leaders had their Bibles out the entire time and were taking copious notes.

At one point during my teaching I asked everyone to open their Bibles to the book of Philippians. There was a woman in the audience who had been reading from her Bible all along, but at this point she turned to the man next to her who didn't have a Bible, and she offered hers to him. I thought it was a gracious offer, but I was curious. So at the break I asked her why she had given her Bible up, and she said, "I didn't need it." I asked why she didn't need it, and she told me that she had memorized the book of Philippians. I was impressed and further intrigued, so I asked her when she had memorized it.

She said, "I was in prison for three years, and I had a lot of free time in prison."

I asked, "They let you have a Bible in prison?"

"No," she said. "Friends would smuggle in pieces of paper with scripture on them. But I had to read fast before the guards found it, so I learned to memorize quickly. Sometimes I would have to eat the paper so that they wouldn't find it."

At the end of the week as our sessions were coming to a close, this same woman spoke up and said, "Brother Joel, would you pray for us? I know you come from America and you have good churches. Pray that we'll become like you."

A level of conviction and sadness came over me in that moment. To think of how many of us have at least three Bibles in our home and never open any of them. To think how many of us neglect the word while a woman in prison is literally consuming scraps of scripture because she's so hungry for the word of God. To think how many of us take for granted attending our air-conditioned churches while these church leaders huddled in a stifling house for a few days of teaching...

I told her, "I can't pray that, but I'll pray this. I'll pray that we will become like you. That God would grant us the same heart and passion you have for his word."

Life Application Questions

1. What simple habit can you start to read your bible more regularly?

2. How can you simplify your bible study?

3. Who can help you better understand the scriptures?

Chapter Seven

Service: The Act of Faith

A while back I had it on my heart to bless my wife in an extra creative way that would totally surprise her. So I decided to cook her dinner.

Maybe that doesn't sound like much to you, but for me, cooking dinner is no small feat. My philosophy around cooking is that it shouldn't take longer to cook a meal than it does to eat that meal. If I weren't married to someone with a different philosophy around cooking, I'd eat scrambled eggs and bread for most meals.

Marie really likes fish, so I decided to cook fish. I bought fish and the makings of a salad, and I put it all in the fridge. Then I stood around the kitchen, not sure what to do next. I opened a couple drawers and then closed them. I peeked into some cabinets. I shuffled around some jars of seasoning. I looked at the recipe I had printed and read through a few of the steps. They had looked easy enough when I had scanned the recipe online, but now that I was actually supposed to follow them, I was totally and completely lost. I got a little cranky and bored and wished I had bought her flowers instead.

I think that's how a lot of us feel when we try to reach out to our neighbors. We have the desire and the vision for it, but when it comes down to the execution, we feel lost and get quickly discouraged.

As I was standing around the kitchen with raw fish in the fridge and no idea what to do next, I knew two things needed to change. I needed a different attitude, and I needed a different strategy. Okay, scratch that. I didn't need a *better* strategy; I needed *any strategy whatsoever*. So I went with the first one that came to my mind. Marie was reading a magazine in another part of the house, and I asked if she wouldn't mind sitting on the couch near the kitchen and continue reading her magazine there. That way if I had questions, I could ask for her help while she continued relaxing. Then I turned on some music, which changed the mood in the kitchen. Once I had a better attitude and strategy, the actual step-by-step tasks of cooking fell into place.

Matthew 9 tells a great story that I think describes the kind of attitude we need to adopt before reaching out to our neighbors. It starts with Jesus spotting Matthew sitting in a tax collector's booth, and saying, "follow me," to which Matthew gets up and follows.

Even though we realize that tax collectors in Jesus' day were a bit shadier than your typical government tax agent today, I don't think we fully realize the kind of complete turn around that Matthew made when he decided to follow Jesus.

A while back I got a phone call from a number I didn't recognize, so I let it go to voicemail. As soon I played the message a few minutes later, my heart dropped. "This is your final call," the voice said. "We're calling to inform you that the IRS has filed a lawsuit against you for default on your taxes."

For thirty seconds I panicked. Then I searched online where I realized that the call was a fraud. The more I read about it, the angrier I got. These people preyed on elderly people and non-citizens, threatening swift penalties and deportation, and then they got people's bank account numbers and emptied their accounts. They made millions of dollars off innocent people. I quickly reported the call and wrote emails and did whatever I could, but I kept thinking about what I would *really* like to do if the person behind the scheme were standing in front of me.

For as bad as that person is, he or she is not nearly as bad as Matthew before meeting Christ.

We see in Matthew 9 that Matthew was sitting in a tax collector's booth. Being a tax collector was bad enough, but the ones that sat in a collector's booth were evil to the core. Matthew didn't just manipulate and make false accusations and commit frauds against strangers in a phonebook—he did all of that against his own people. And yet Jesus found him and called him out, and Matthew left his lucrative, sinful life and followed Jesus.

Immediately after, Matthew had Jesus and the disciples over to his house for dinner, and he invited all of his tax collector friends to join them. The disciples and Jesus were mingling with all of these known sinners who would never be seen near a synagogue. It was like a sinner and savior mixer, if you will. I imagine Matthew was in some kind of surreal, satisfied state of mind, watching his old life and his new life collide and seeing Jesus minister to his old friends.

But partway through the evening, the Pharisees show up. They try planting a seed of doubt and self-righteousness in the disciples' minds by asking them, "Why does your teacher eat with tax collectors and sinners?" Jesus overhears them and corrects them—I think for the disciples' sake more so than for the Pharisees'. He was coaching the disciples in the kind of attitude they needed to have in those situations. He reminded them that it's not the healthy who need a doctor, but the sick. He quotes Hosea, saying that he desires mercy, not sacrifice. It's not about the outward display of religion but about the condition of their hearts.

Loving our neighbors is not a task that we can measure by outward displays of religious sacrifice. We're called to love our neighbors, not to fix our neighbors. Let's not get confused; Jesus is the doctor who came for the sick, not us. Our job is simply to reflect God's love.

Once we adopt an attitude of love, then it's time for a strategy.

I think the most clear and straightforward explanation of the strategy Jesus demonstrated in his ministry comes from Paul in 1 Corinthians 9, starting in verse 19.

Though I am free and belong to no one, I have made myself a slave to everyone, to win as many as possible. To the Jews I became like a Jew, to win the Jews. To those under the law I became like one under the law (though I myself am not under the law), so as to win those under the law. To those not having the law I became like one not having the law (though I am not free from God's law but am under Christ's law), so as to win those not having the law. To the weak I became weak, to win the weak. I have become all things to all people so that by all possible means I might save some. I do all this for the sake of the gospel, that I may share in its blessings."

Look again at the first verse, because therein lies the strategy. "Though I am free and belong to no one, I have made myself a slave to everyone, to win as many as possible." God's strategy is simple. Serve people.

Paul was a very intelligent and highly influential person. In his day there was a position called "sophos," which was essentially like having a PhD in wisdom. Some of Paul's people were encouraging him to acquire the status because they thought it would increase his place in society and make him more influential. He would have more authority and superiority, and he would be better able to accomplish his mission.

But Paul tells them they have it all wrong. The way to influence is through service. Jesus' mission is not going to be accomplished through superstars. God's strategy is servanthood, not fame. The method has to match the message, and the message is love and service.

Have you ever seen a mom yell at her kids to stop yelling at each other? Or, worse, have you ever seen a parent hit a child because the child hit someone else? They're not matching the method with the message. If the gospel is love, we're not going to get it across through harshness and superiority. The Bible says that the light of the gospel shines when we serve with good deeds.

There's a great story in the New Testament that demonstrates this to an incredible degree. Paul is in prison in chains, and suddenly the chains fall off and the doors to the jail are opened. Paul has been supernaturally set free from prison. But what does he do? He stays in prison. If he gets up and walks out, the guard responsible for him would lose his job or worse. So he stays in prison out of sacrificial service to this guard. What an almost *unfathomable* good deed. The guard sees what Paul did for him, and he asks what he needs to do to be saved. It wasn't the miracle of the jail door opening that convinced him of his need for a savior; it was Paul's sacrificial kindness.

I once met a woman in China who was arrested for evangelizing, and the jailor told her that if she paid a bribe, he would let her go. She knew she didn't have the money for the bribe, but when she reached her hand in her pocket, she found the exact amount of money that had been demanded for a bribe. God supernaturally provided a way out of prison for her. What did she do? She put the money back in her pocket, curious at how God was going to use that money for his Kingdom. When she told me this story, I remember thinking, *what?* God provides exactly what you need to get out of prison at exactly the time you need it, and you're curious what he's up to?

In prison she met three prostitutes who had been beaten and abused, and she had an opportunity to pray with them to receive Jesus before using her money to free them. She sent them off to her village, where members of her home church ministered to them and discipled them. The money that could have bought her freedom, she used to buy the freedom of these three girls.

Those are profound examples of sacrificial kindness that can change lives in one powerful moment. But what about smaller, more day-to-day good deeds?

One day I saw an elderly man carrying some grocery bags, so I pulled my car over and asked him if I could help. He accepted, and we walked to his house around the corner, not really saying much. I set the grocery bags down on his kitchen table and was ready to leave when he asked me, "Why did you stop to help me?" I had the opportunity to tell him how there was once a time in my life when I didn't care about anyone but myself, but that God's love had transformed me, and that now I live to show others that same love. Did he fall to his knees and ask, "What do I need to do in order to be saved?" No. But I got to plant a seed. Whenever you serve someone, you plant a seed.

The core of Paul's strategy lies in that first verse about servanthood ("I became a slave to everyone"). But then Paul goes into more detail about how he serves people. In order to serve people, he becomes like them in order to identify with them. I think another way to put that would be that Paul was so confident in his identity in Christ that he never lost sight of who he was no matter what situation he was in. He could relate to people on any level and in any circumstance. If that sounds too complicated, then try this: just be genuine, and don't lose sight of who you are in Christ. Don't try to be perfect or have all the answers. Don't try to be a professional Christian. Just be who you are. Be authentic.

As a missionary kid in South Korea, my early life was a bit sheltered and one-dimensional. People think that missionary kids come home from the field with this expansive worldview and global experience that kids raised in America don't have, which is true. But it's also true that I lacked the experience and knowledge the kids raised in America had, even though America was technically my home country. That's just part of the complexity of being a TCK (third culture kid).

When I first moved to the States at age 18 to go to college, I was living in a house with a group of guys. The guy who lived across the street from us didn't take care of his rental house or lawn at all. He even had random car parts that were strewn around the lawn.

One day I was mowing our front lawn wondering why my neighbor never cleaned up his yard. I was getting a bit angry with him when I sense that God showed me that I had a lawnmower and my neighbor had a lawn that needing mowing. So, I went across the street and mowed his yard. Whenever I came to a car part or piece of metal, I mowed carefully around it. The end result was a perfectly manicured lawn with random patches of tall grass in the shapes of car parts. Then I left the lawn mower on the front side of my house for him to see it. I hoped he would notice that I was the one who had mowed his lawn and come over to thank me. Then I could witness to him.

However, when he pulled in his driveway later that day, I watched out my window as he got out of his truck, took a quick glance around, and walked inside. He went to work the next morning, came home that afternoon, got out of is car, and didn't even look at his lawn before going into his house. It drove me crazy! So when I saw him outside later that afternoon, I walked across the street.

"Hey, I see your lawn is mowed," I said.

"Yeah, did you do that?" he asked. I nodded. Then I said, "You probably should move these pieces of metal and car parts."

He said, "I'd love to be able to move them, but I injured my back a few weeks ago and I can't lift them myself." I groaned to myself for how quick I had been to judge him without knowing his story. I told him I would be happy to help him move these metal parts. He said he wanted to move the pieces to the dump on the other side of town, so I helped lift them into the back of his truck. Once we are both sitting in the truck, he lit up a joint.

Now, it was freezing outside, so I didn't know what to do. Should I roll down the window? Was I going to get high off all the smoke that was filling the truck cab? Then he started talking, and he used two words that I'd never heard before: "toke" and "reefer." I had to decide what to do. I could fake that I was comfortable and go along with it, or I could get holier than thou and make it clear I didn't approve of him. Neither of those choices would help me befriend him or be a witness to him. I had a third option. I could simply be genuine. So I looked at him and said, "I have no idea what you're talking about. Something about a refill?"

He replied to me, "Really dude? You don't know what a reefer is? Why not?"

I explained that I was a missionary kid and was still new to the States. Then it was his turn to be confused—he had no idea what a missionary kid was. We sort of bonded over the fact that we didn't understand each other at all, and we ended up having this great, open, honest conversation. A few years later I found out that he became a Christian and was attending a church.

When it comes to loving your neighbors, count the conversations, not the conversions. Some plant, some water, and some harvest. But every opportunity to genuinely love and serve your neighbor falls somewhere in that process. And you can't genuinely serve your neighbor unless you are genuinely yourself with them.

So, once we have the attitude and the strategy in place, there's still one thing missing. We still need action steps. I'm in the kitchen, I'm humming along the music, I've got my wife on the couch to help me, I have all the ingredients...but I still have to execute it all, step by step.

Romans 15:3 says, "Each of us should reach his neighbor for his good to build him up." I use the word R.E.A.C.H. as an acronym for five very practical, sequential steps for reaching our neighbors.

R: Ready your heart.

Specifically, identify five names of people who you think God has put on your heart to reach. They could be coworkers or someone from your kids' school or actual neighbors down the street. But write down five names.

Then, start praying for them. When you start praying for someone, your heart becomes attune to that person, and God can begin sharing his heart for that person with you.

E: Engage through kindness.

While you're praying for the names on your list, start asking God for ideas. How can you show these people love and kindness? Keep this part simple. Don't do something outrageous—do something that they can easily accept without embarrassment. Find a way to serve them without making a big show of it.

A: Advance to relationship.

Say you find some way to serve all five people on your list. Most likely everyone will be grateful in some way, but for one or two of them, something richer will take place. There will be an extra conversation or extra depth to your engagement with them, and you'll see that God is doing something particular with that person through you. Remember, you're not orchestrating this. You're just taking simple action steps and following God's lead from there.

My wife and I did this when we lived in our neighborhood where we were trying to become friends with eight couples. We wanted to reach them and find a way to invite them to church, so we started with these acts of kindness. There was one couple, more than any of the other couples, who we immediately were able to have a more in depth friendship with. They began to ask us about our faith, so when it came time to invite people to church, we invited this one couple who agreed to come. But on that

Sunday they did not come alone. They had gone and invited all the other couples, I think for fear of not wanting to attend church by themselves. So on that Sunday, all the couples from our neighborhood showed up to hear me preach.

My wife and I were so amazed to watch God at work.

C: Connect to church.

Did you know that 80 percent of Americans who are invited to a church say yes? Maybe they say yes because it would be awkward to say no, but they still say yes! Only 20 percent say no. If you had those odds in Vegas, you'd be a millionaire. So if you invite five people to church, statistically speaking, four of them are going to say yes. And even if one or some say no, you have still taken a great step, because now your faith is an open conversation in your relationship with them. So, "yes" is a win and "no" is a win; the only answer that's not a win is silence. It's always best to invite people face-to-face and its even better to bring them to church. Make an event out of it and share a meal with them after the service.

Why is connecting your neighbor to church important? A local church is going to be the best support in your process of sharing God's love with your neighbor. It's something that you get to experience with them that will open up opportunities for conversation with them later. They'll get to see what a community of Christ-followers looks like. They'll hear teaching and scripture, and they'll meet other Christians. Especially if you've been having conversations about faith with your neighbors, bringing them to church will lend credibility to those conversations, because they'll see that it's not just you. There's a whole community of people who are participating in this way of life that you're talking about.

H: Hand over to God.

This is an important final step. It's important to have the right attitude and strategy, and it's important to take action, but once you do all of those things, it's tempting to carry a burden that you're not intended to carry. It is not your job to convince anyone or to "close the deal." Count the conversations, not the conversions. Look at these five people with a spirit of love. Just relax and have faith. Trust Jesus to work in them.

My church has a ministry called Work Life, where hundreds of our marketplace leaders come together and discuss what it means to influence the marketplace for Christ. One Friday night, at the end of the meeting, a man named James came up and introduced himself to me. He told me that he had been attending the church for four months, and I asked who had invited him. It turns out no one had invited him. He had gone through a couple of rough years and wanted to reconnect with the Lord, so he started coming to our church on his own accord and got involved. He told me he was signing up to get baptized soon.

James's story is rare, but it can happen. God can absolutely work on people's hearts without our help. But for whatever reason, he generally chooses to work through us. I think the reason has something to do with the fact that, as he's working through us, he's also working in us.

My wife really was amazed by the dinner I cooked for her. I set the table, lit candles and turned on soft music for our dinner. Incredibly, the fish turned out just right, and I managed not to ruin the salad. But as moved as she was by my act of service, I was so excited that I got to provide that experience for her and show love to her in this special way.

And that's only a small picture of what God wants to deposit in you as you reach your neighbors with his love.

Life Application Questions

1. Who is your neighbor to REACH?

2. Why is it hard to reach your neighbor?

3. How does serving change when you define it as reaching your neighbor?

Conclusion

Faith was never designed by God to be a struggle. A relationship with God was never designed to be difficult and confusing. Faith is meant to be simple, not complicated. These seven basic building blocks of faith are essential to building a relationship with God, but they should be alive and exciting not merely theological ideas.

Being chosen is the greatest gift, giving value to each of us. Experiencing God's grace transforms us. Community humbles us as we admit that we cannot live in faith on our own. Worship inspires us as we fulfill our created purpose. Prayer empowers us as the Spirit of God is at work within us. Studying the Scriptures gives us wisdom as we discover truth. Service blesses us as we become like God when we give ourselves away. These seven foundations of faith, when prioritized and practiced, engage us with a living God, waiting for us to believe Him in every dimension of life.

See. Faith. Different. is the second in a series of three books. The first, See. Life. Different examines the seven basic building blocks of daily life. The last, See. God. Different. will examine the seven aspects of God's character, often unrecognizable to us. But without See. Faith. Different., the other two volumes are meaningless. For without faith it is impossible to please God. It is impossible to know God. It is impossible to live with God. See faith different and live a full and complete life with God.

ABOUT THE AUTHOR

Joel Holm is a life-long learner and a strategic thinker who has always wanted to make the world a better place, especially for the weak and the vulnerable. Motivated by his faith, Joel has a passion to help corporations, churches and civic organizations make a genuine, long-lasting impact through creative initiatives. Joel has two earned graduated degrees in Theology and Education but more than anything he simply considers himself a follower of Jesus. Joel has written numerous books, traveled to more than 90 countries, and seen God and faith at work in countless environments. From his vast and unique experiences, Joel brings a wealth of insight and learning to every forum in which he speaks and leads. Joel is most grateful that he gets to share his adventurous life with his wife, Marie, and their children.

To contact Joel and access additional resources visit
Joelholm.com

Joel Holm

Made in the USA
San Bernardino, CA
11 July 2017